Textual Knowledge

Teaching the Bible
in Theory and in Practice

A person . . . can bring to the Bible only a readiness both for belief and for unbelief, not a circumscribable belief that he finds the Bible confirming. Even his readiness is uncircumscribed and unlimited. Everything can become credible for him, even the incredible. . . . Not everything in Scripture belongs to him, not today and not ever. But he knows that he belongs to all of it. This readiness and this readiness alone is, as applied to Scripture, his belief.

From Franz Rosenzweig, "Scripture and Luther," in Martin Buber and Franz Rosenzweig, *Scripture and Translation,* trans. Lawrence Rosenwald with Everett Fox (Bloomington: Indiana University Press, 1994), pp. 58–59.

He must face the Book with a new attitude as something new. He must yield to it, withhold nothing of his being, and let whatever will occur between himself and it. He does not know which of its sayings and images will overwhelm him and mold him, from where the spirit will ferment and enter into him, to incorporate itself anew in his body. But he holds himself open.

From Martin Buber, "The Man of Today and the Jewish Bible," in his collection *On the Bible,* ed. Nahum N. Glatzer (New York: Schocken, 1968), p. 5.

Perhaps instead of thinking about the Bible as a book to be deciphered, or a story to be told, we should think of it as a person. We do not decipher people, we encounter them. And the closer we are to a person the more certain we will be that we cannot tell his story.

From Gabriel Josipovici, *The Book of God: A Response to the Bible* (New Haven: Yale University Press, 1988), p. 307.

Textual Knowledge

Teaching the Bible
in Theory and in Practice

Barry W. Holtz

The Jewish Theological Seminary of America

This book is dedicated to my children,
Sophia and Elan
May their study of Torah enrich their lives

Jewish Education Series, Volume 1

Contents

Introduction

This is a book about teaching the Bible. The context is Jewish education, though I would define that phrase quite broadly: Jewish education means, as one might expect, day schools and synagogue schools, but it also means adult education, informal education, and even university settings, at least at the undergraduate level. Curiously enough, the process of writing this book over the past few years has taught me something about the way that people think about Jewish education, or perhaps about education in general: I found that whenever I told people that I was working on a book about teaching the Bible, I was struck by how often I received the following response: "And you're gearing this for teachers of what age students?"

The response is not surprising. We hear "teaching," and immediately we think of learning. We think "teacher," and naturally we think "student." But the immediate move to the practical, the quick assumption that writing a book about the Bible means *by necessity* that you have a focus on a specific set of students, was something that was almost universal.

To be sure, the question "who are the students" also points to one of the features of teaching that contemporary educational researchers most emphasize: that teaching is not something that takes place in a world of generalities. Rather, teaching is a highly "specified" enterprise requiring knowledge that is unique to the particular discipline being taught;[1] and it is highly specified in terms of the learners involved in any given situation. We picture a Bible teacher with young children or a scholar with advanced graduate students and we understand that the pedagogy in both cases is extraordinarily different. In addition, teaching, in the language of educational scholarship, is an example of "situated knowledge."[2] No one teaches in a decontextualized environment—there is always teaching of *this* particular subject in *that* particular context to *those* particular students.

Yet, at the same time, the immediate move to "teachers of which students" also speaks of a different kind of impulse, the move to think about education as an *activity before we think of it as an intellectual enterprise;* before we spend five minutes thinking about the *content* of teaching, we are already thinking about the enactment of teaching.

What if we began a different way and asked, "How shall we think about the subject matters we teach?" And here I mean both those subjects as academic disciplines and those same disciplines as we think about them for *teaching.* As I will try to show during the course of this book, these two concerns, though closely related, are not one thing. How we think about the particular content—whether it be mathematics, literature, or Bible—and how we think about it as *teachers* are two different enterprises. We all recognize that there are experts in disciplines, "people who are fluent in a subject."[3] These experts

> are distinguished from others in at least three respects: (1) they know a great deal of specific content, that is, facts and ideas; (2) they have formed a variety of complex relationships among these pieces of content; and (3) they understand how to approach new problems or dilemmas and how to produce new ideas within the subject.[4]

Yet we also know that there is a big difference between what it means to be an expert who knows one's subject matter in order "to practice in the discipline" and what it means to be a teacher who knows a subject in order "to make connections between what he or she understands and what students bring to the lesson."[5]

In this book, my concern will be with the Bible, though the questions I will pose could be asked of any academic area. The answers, however, in all their specificity, will be bound up with the Bible as text, as academic discipline, as school subject in the world of Jewish education.

For most of my adult life, I have been a teacher. Nowadays I teach graduate students and rabbinical students; thirty years ago, I taught junior high schoolers and high schoolers. These have been the students whom I've taught in "school" settings, but there have been other students as well—adults in synagogues and Jewish community centers wanting learning for the sake of learning, teachers and school principals in professional development sessions, home study groups, and even one-on-one tutoring.

Throughout it all, humming in the background, has been the Bible, for even though I've taught other aspects of Jewish literature, history, and religion, in the end one always comes back to the Bible. There is no avoiding it. The Bible is such a core text, both for Western culture as a whole and for the smaller arena of Jewish education, the area within which I spend most of my time, that it needs no justification as an area of educational concern. And, indeed, there are many textbooks that have been developed for Bible teaching.[6]

But my concern here is not with creating detailed lessons for teaching the Bible, but rather with trying to think about the larger issues involved in Bible teaching: What are our purposes? How do we conceptualize the Bible as a subject matter? How do we develop theories of Bible teaching? And how do we move from theory to practice?

The question of the relationship between theory and practice has long perplexed those involved in "practical" disciplines such as education.[7] In these domains, theory and practice are often seen as conflictive or oppositional. Theory, it is believed, lives in the world of abstract concepts; practice is about getting things done in the "real world." As Wilfred Carr puts it, people believe that "solutions to theoretical problems are found in knowing something; practical problems can only be solved by doing something."[8] But Carr points out that there is a problem applying this view to the area of education:

> When applied to the field of education, however, this view of practice is always unsatisfactory. For example, certain educational problems (What should I teach? What should I include in the "core" curriculum?) are clearly "practical" in the sense that they are problems about what to do. At the same time, however, they are "general" rather than "particular," "abstract" rather than "concrete," and relatively "context-free."[9]

At the same time, there are many educational issues in which "the practical situation may call for immediate action based on a timeless question that has been debated 'in theory' since the time of Plato."[10] Deciding the specific content of the Bible curriculum for students of different abilities may raise enduring questions about the nature and value of human beings, the role of intelligence in evaluating individuals, and the justice of evaluation entirely.

As Carr points out, "by making the twin assumptions that all practice is non-theoretical and all theory is non-practical, this approach [of seeing theory and practice as oppositional] always underestimates the extent to which those who engage in educational practices have to reflect upon, and hence theorize about, what in general they are trying to do."[11]

As a teacher of the Bible, I am embedded in a world of choice. I am aware that "practice is itself always particular and has to take account of the changing conditions under which it has to operate."[12] I am challenged by the specific needs of my students, by the context in which I am working, and by the nature of the subject matter itself. Because I believe that in the world of education, theory and practice are interactive rather than oppositional, my ideas about the biggest issues that I can imagine are inevitably related to the way they will be worked out in practice. To improve my practice, I might think about "methods" of teaching, or activities to do with my students, but if I don't explore the theoretical dimensions of my work, my attempt to work on my practice is likely to fail.

In this book, I want to concentrate on two important components of theory necessary for the practice of teaching the Bible. One aspect is our underlying goals: What are our purposes in teaching the Bible? What are the outcomes that we are looking for? In what way do we "justify"[13] the enterprise of teaching the Bible? Too often, the issue of goals is ignored in thinking about teaching, particularly in the arena of Jewish education. Indeed, Seymour Fox has argued that "the most urgent problem facing Jewish education today is its lack of purpose and, consequently, its blandness."[14] In his view, only a serious philosophical deliberation about the goals of education can address this crisis. In this book, I will try to explore the purposes of teaching the Bible, looking both at alternative views and at some of the difficulties that teachers might encounter in implementing their goals.

My second area of focus will be on the relationship between *knowledge* of Bible and *teaching* the Bible. What kind of knowledge does the Bible teacher need to have? How must that knowledge of subject matter be structured and conceptualized? How must "knowledge be held in a form that enables it to be reshaped depending on the kinds of ideas students bring up in a discussion or in the activity of trying to solve a problem"?[15] How might differing scholarly conceptions of the discipline influence teachers' ways of thinking about the Bible? Drawing upon recent research in the field of general education, I draw connections to the domain of Bible education.

This book is called *Textual Knowledge* because I believe that dealing with the issue of a teacher's knowledge of the subject matter and the relationship of that knowledge to both teaching goals and instructional methods is the most important starting point for improving pedagogy—making it deeper, richer, more reflective, and more powerful for students. I am a Jewish educator, and my focus will emerge out of that perspective, but I believe that the issues I raise here are relevant to educators from other religious traditions and for educators teaching the Bible in secular institutions such as universities as well.

•　　•　　•

The book begins with a chapter that investigates the difficulties of teaching sacred literature—particularly the Bible and other Jewish texts—in contemporary American culture. The chapter explores some examples of these difficulties, particularly the pseudo-religious images embedded within popular culture, as exemplified in recent Disney animated movies. The chapter locates the roots and tenacity of such images in the version of "American religion" most often associated with the writings of Ralph Waldo Emerson.

Chapter 2 begins with an exploration of the problem of goals in education and explores the way that different goals lead to a variety of practices in the real life of classrooms. The work of Joseph Schwab, Lee Shulman, and particularly Pamela Grossman is explored to see its important implications for Jewish education. Grossman's work looks at the teaching of English literature, and by applying some of her categories and approaches, we find ways to relate this body of work to teaching the Bible.

Chapter 3 develops a "map" of possible approaches to teaching the Bible, rooted both in contemporary biblical scholarship and in the "wisdom of practice" from the field. In what way is academic scholarship about Bible relevant to the *teaching* of Bible? In what way can the work of teachers in the field and curriculum materials form the basis of a theory of teaching Bible? Joseph Schwab's work on the structure of disciplines forms the backbone of our theoretical perspective, but Schwab's work is also challenged for its limitations in dealing with the unique qualities of the Bible and the specific context of Jewish education. The chapter begins by looking at three possible approaches to the teaching of English literature and, building on that investigation, moves toward the implications for teaching the Bible. The chapter concludes with a theoretical map identifying nine pedagogical orientations to the Bible.

Chapter 4 leads us to a consideration of the *goals* of teaching the Bible. How does one move from the notion of orientations to the overarching purposes that we have for teaching? There are a number of different possible goals for teaching the Bible, including the inherent interest of the text and, for others, the sense of religious obligation that a person may feel to study these words. In this chapter, however, I spend most of the time exploring the idea of "the Bible as truth." Using the work of a variety of philosophers, theologians, and literary theorists (including Hans-Georg Gadamer, Martin Buber, Michael Fishbane, Martha Nussbaum, and Wayne C. Booth), I try to tease out the educational implications of viewing the Bible as a text that communicates "truth."

To say that we can view "truth" as one goal for the teaching of the Bible does not answer other difficulties that the teacher is likely to encounter. Perhaps most pressing is the problem of "troubling texts," sections of the Bible that teachers might find difficult to deal with. Our difficulties may stem from a variety of sources, including, most importantly, the great distance in time between our world and the world of the Bible. Chapter 5 tries to examine this essential problem. What does a teacher do about texts that he or she finds "difficult"? I begin the chapter by looking at Dante's *Inferno* as an example of a classic text and suggest ways in which that text might be read as an exploration about the nature of teachers and students. But what does it mean to do what I set out to do in that reading—to use an "old" text for contemporary interpretations? I move from there to a close examination of specific difficulties that may be raised by the use of such texts and examine five approaches to dealing with such difficulties. The chapter concludes with a look at philosophical attempts to "translate" wisdom from one context to another.

Finally, chapter 6 looks at issues behind the preparation of Bible teachers and proposes different ways to help teachers think about using their knowledge to prepare for their classes. In particular, I am interested in helping teachers use various resources, including contemporary biblical scholarship, as a way of concentrating on "what's worth learning" in whatever texts they choose to teach. That investigation leads to a consideration of implementing Lee Shulman's notion of "pedagogical content knowledge" through a series of exercises related specifically to teaching the Bible. I conclude by proposing one model for prospective teachers or experienced teachers in professional development programs to use a combination of their own knowledge, focused work with Bible scholars, and interaction with real classrooms, students, and teachers to help improve their own practice.

•   •   •

As will be obvious to any careful reader, this book owes a great deal to a number of intellectual mentors who have influenced my thinking. To mention them all would fill another entire book! I have been blessed with a number of great teachers in my life, from a variety of different disciplines, and their symbolic fingerprints might easily be discerned by a sleuth with a watchful eye. These teachers might be found in actual classrooms and study halls or in the pages of books that have influenced me. Some have become friends; others I have never met. I want to try to single out a few of the most obvious suspects, with apologies to the many who go unnamed but are deeply appreciated.

In the world of Jewish education, I want to single out three individuals. If it were not for Joe Lukinsky, I would never have ended up as a Jewish educator or a professor of Jewish education. I often wonder, in fact, how much of a committed and involved Jew I would have become if it were not for him. I met Joe when I was in the seventh or eighth grade, and he became for me, and a whole group of friends, a model of rabbi, teacher, and moral individual. It was my great privilege to end up serving on the same faculty with him at the Jewish Theological Seminary many years after we first met. He is surely one of the most creative minds that we have seen in our field, and I am thankful for the opportunity that I have had to learn from him.

I met Seymour Fox thanks in part to Joe, and Seymour's way of thinking about Jewish education clearly informs the pages of this book. He became my unofficial postdoctoral teacher, and it was through Seymour that I came to the Seminary, originally at the Melton Research Center, later to join the faculty. It remains an enduring pleasure to work with him and to continue to learn from his insights.

Finally, I want to mention a wonderful Jewish educator who became my teacher by being my colleague. I've worked with Gail Dorph first at the Melton Research Center (where I was her "boss"—the quotation marks are quite intentional), then at the Council for Initiatives in Jewish Education, and, most recently, at the Mandel Foundation's Teacher Educator Institute. Our weekly—sometimes daily—conversations about issues of teaching and learning the Bible have informed much of my thinking. That ongoing dialogue is found in these pages.

Other friends in and around Jewish education have been particularly helpful and encouraging in a variety of ways. These include: Alan Hoffmann, Mike Rosenak, Nessa Rapoport, along with my colleagues in the Seminary's Department of Jewish Education, and my students over many years, particularly in my "Teaching Texts" course at the Seminary and in the "Curriculum Theory" course that I taught at the Hebrew University during 1997–98. Sadly, my dear friend and colleague Edy Rauch did not live to see the publication of this volume. He was a steadfast supporter of my intellectual work and I am deeply saddened by the loss of his wise presence.

I also want to mention those wise and insightful scholars outside of the world of Jewish education who have helped me think about my own field in different ways and whose research is felt in these pages. In particular, I want to single out scholars from general education whose work is closely allied to the ideas found in this book: most of all to Sharon Feiman-Nemser and Deborah Ball, from whom I've learned so much during our work together at the Teacher Educator Institute.

In addition, I want to mention two teachers from years ago whose insights into literature and literary theory helped inspire some of the thinking in this book: Allen Grossman and Jesper Rosenmeier.

There have been many Bible scholars and Bible teachers whom I've had a chance to learn from and talk with over the years. Scholars, experts in curriculum, classroom teachers—all have helped me refine my thinking about these matters. I want to especially thank two friends with whom I had a chance to talk and study on a regular basis in Jerusalem during the year that the bulk of this work was written: George Savran and Noam Zion. Others include: Ed Greenstein, Ruth Zielenziger, Yair Zakovitch, and Michael Fishbane.

I owe a debt of gratitude to a number of institutions for their support during the past four years of work. I am grateful for the sabbatical leave from my home base, the Jewish Theological Seminary, which allowed me to spend a year in Israel working primarily on this project and to the Mr. Earle Kazis Publication Fund which helped make this volume possible. While in Israel, I received additional support from other institutions: the Mandel Foundation, where I was privileged to be named the first visiting Mandel Fellow; the Mandel School—in particular, the Jerusalem Fellows program there; and the Hebrew University's

Melton Centre for Jewish Education in the Diaspora. Many thanks to the people who made my stay so pleasant at all these places, especially: Annette Hochstein, Howie Deitcher, Ze'ev Mankowitz, and Seymour Fox, who has been mentioned above.

I want to thank Alan Cooper and the other members of the Publications Committee at the Jewish Theological Seminary Press for so enthusiastically taking on this project. Their suggestions and those of the two anonymous outside readers have helped me improve the manuscript and sharpen this book's focus.

Finally, my greatest debt of gratitude goes to my family, whose loving support was essential during this time: my wife, Bethamie Horowitz, whose own groundbreaking work on issues of Jewish identity helps locate the enterprise of Jewish education; and my two children, Sophia and Elan, whose own adventures in learning the Bible help bring all of this to life and to whom this book is dedicated.

Notes

1. See Paul Hirst, "Liberal Education and the Nature of Knowledge," in his collection of papers, *Knowledge and the Curriculum* (London and Boston: Routledge & Kegan Paul, 1974). On subject-specific pedagogy: Mary Kennedy, *Trends and Issues in Teachers' Subject Matter Knowledge* (Washington, D.C.: ERIC Clearinghouse on Teacher Education, 1990); G. Williamson McDiarmid, Deborah Loewenberg Ball, and Charles W. Anderson, "Why Staying One Chapter Ahead Doesn't Really Work: Subject-Specific Pedagogy," in *Knowledge Base for the Beginning Teacher,* ed. M. Reynolds (New York: Pergamon, 1989); and Susan S. Stodolsky, *The Subject Matters* (Chicago: University of Chicago Press, 1988).

2. Sharon Feiman-Nemser and Janine Remillard, "Perspectives on Learning to Teach," in *The Teacher Educator's Handbook,* ed. Frank B. Murray (San Francisco: Jossey-Bass, 1996), pp. 81–85; Jean Lave and Etienne Wenger, *Situated Learning* (Cambridge: Cambridge University Press, 1991); and Paul Cobb and Janet Bowers, "Cognitive and Situated Learning Perspectives in Theory and Practice," *Educational Researcher* 28, no. 2 (1999): 4–15.

3. Kennedy, *Trends and Issues,* p. 7.

4. Ibid.

5. Ruth M. Heaton and Magdalene Lampert, "Learning to Hear Voices: Inventing a New Pedagogy of Teacher Education," in *Teaching for Understanding: Challenges for Policy and Practice,* ed. David K. Cohen, Milbrey W. McLaughlin, and Joan E. Talbert (San Francisco: Jossey-Bass, 1993), p. 54.

6. Within Jewish education alone, one could point to Seymour Rossel, *A Child's*

Bible (West Orange, N.J.: Behrman House, 1988); Ruth Zielenziger, teachers' guides to Genesis and Exodus, published by the Melton Research Center, 1979, 1984, respectively; and Joel Grishaver's *Being Torah* (Los Angeles: Tora Aura, 1986).

7. Chris Argyris and Donald A. Schön, *Theory in Practice* (San Francisco: Jossey-Bass, 1974).

8. Wilfred Carr, "What Is an Educational Practice?" *Journal of Philosophy of Education* 21, no. 2 (1987): 164.

9. Ibid.

10. Ibid.

11. Ibid.

12. Ibid., p. 170.

13. On justification, see Israel Scheffler, "Justifying Curriculum Decisions," in his *Reason and Teaching* (London: Routledge & Kegan Paul, 1973); and R. S. Peters, "The Justification of Education," in his *Education and the Education of Teachers* (London: Routledge & Kegan Paul, 1977).

14. Seymour Fox, "Toward a General Theory of Jewish Education," in *The Future of the American Jewish Community,* ed. David Sidorsky (New York: Basic Books, 1973); also Fox's "From Theory to Practice in Jewish Education" (paper presented at the Twelfth World Congress of Jewish Studies, Jerusalem, 30 July 1997). In addition, Daniel Pekarsky, "The Place of Vision in Jewish Educational Reform," *Journal of Jewish Education* 63, nos. 1–2 (winter/spring 1997): 31–40.

15. Heaton and Lampert, "Learning to Hear Voices," p. 54.

CHAPTER ONE

Teaching Religious Texts
in the Landscape of America

In the midst of the social unrest of the late 1960s, the American poet and literary theorist Allen Grossman delivered a provocative talk entitled "Teaching Literature in a Discredited Civilization."[1] Grossman's theme was the relationship between education and what he viewed as a corrupt and dangerous culture, and although his focus was far different from what I will be exploring here, his title brings to mind the often unexplored relationship between the world in which we teach and the world in which we live. This issue has a particular resonance for teachers of Jewish texts in the Diaspora who live as part of a minority culture represented by the books that they teach and who live, as well, as part of a general culture whose values and beliefs may run counter to that which they are teaching.

In what way does our culture shape, direct, or influence our teaching of texts like the Bible? In what way are we required to reframe our conception of those texts? Indeed, one might ask: In what way do our texts get "rewritten" by living in the non-Jewish culture? Or, to use another language, How can we *teach* the Lord's song in a strange land? Nor is this problem only that of the "strange lands" of the Diaspora, though it may be felt more keenly there. How much is contemporary, secular, Israeli culture a hospitable home for the texts of the tradition, particularly the postbiblical sources?

In the field of education, the area that we are looking at goes by a number of names. Lawrence Cremin, for example, speaks about the numerous educating institutions in any community as forming an "ecology" of education.[2] Ralph Tyler describes the need to investigate "contemporary life outside the school" when embarking on any curriculum project.[3]

For Joseph Schwab, the term is "the milieus," which he identified as one of the "commonplaces"[4] inherent in any educational situation.[5] Note Schwab's use of the plural—for any individual student, milieus are multiple. They include the specific educational setting—in the world of formal education, it is the individual classroom and beyond that the school as a whole; in informal education, it might be the summer camp or an organized educational trip. Milieus expand to include the child's family, synagogue, and larger community. And eventually, they include the entire national culture in which the child resides. These ultimately are circles within circles, ranging, one might say, from milieu with a lowercase *m* to Milieu with a capital letter—the culture as a whole. The question for education, as Schwab states it, is: "What are the conditions, dominant preoccupations, and cultural climate of the whole polity and its social classes, insofar as they may affect the careers, the probable fate, and ego identity of the children whom we want to teach?"[6]

We might represent graphically the situation as follows:

Four Types of "Milieu"

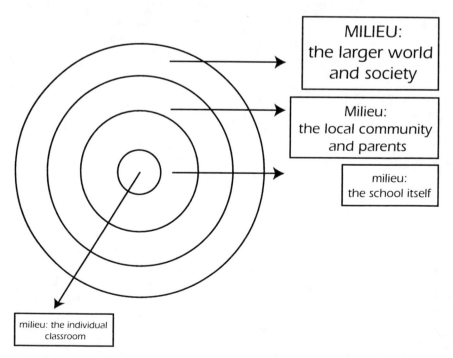

MILIEU:
the larger world
and society

Milieu:
the local community
and parents

milieu:
the school itself

milieu: the individual
classroom

Although Schwab raises milieu as an important element in any curricular deliberation, "it is unfortunate," as Seymour Fox points out, "that Schwab did not develop this topic more extensively."[7] Indeed, as Fox goes on to show, Schwab's later work seems to turn away from issues of the larger culture. Thus, instead of using social scientists in his process of curricular deliberation, as he had suggested earlier in his career, Schwab came to focus on school-based partners such as principals and parents. The largest circle in the drawing above, in other words, became over time less and less important in Schwab's presentation of the curriculum process. In doing so, "Schwab appears to be avoiding the question that Tyler asks about the needs of the larger contemporary society as well as about the demands that are likely to be made on the student by society in the future."[8]

Fox is certainly correct here, but his focus on "needs" and "demands" may emphasize too much the positive dimensions of the larger milieu. The undermining, perhaps even corrupting, aspects of the larger society play a significant role in the contemporary challenges of Jewish education. After all, Milieu with a large M is that commonplace least under the control of educators, excluding perhaps the ultraorthodox community (though even within that community, the influence of the outside, larger culture is not to be underestimated).[9] And partially for that very reason, "Milieu writ large" may be the greatest challenge that Jewish educators must face. The power of milieu has an impact on Jewish teaching in a number of significant ways. How these matters affect the way we teach texts like the Bible in America today will be my concern here.

The tension between the ideas of the classical Jewish tradition and the "acceptable" values of modern American culture is one of the primary issues faced by Jewish educators. To put it baldly: How does one teach the Jewish tradition faithfully and accurately when those teachings may conflict with the mainstream culture in which our students live?

There are times, of course, in which the nature of this conflict resembles that described by Allen Grossman in the talk mentioned above. In such cases, the mainstream culture is so morally bankrupt, so corrupted, that any connection between that culture and the Jewish tradition seems unimaginable. Indeed, this is the very view of modernity inherent in contemporary ultraorthodoxy.[10] But it is not only fundamentalist separatists who may sense such a conflict. The British educator Peter Abbs expresses a different version of the same critique. He is worried about the impact of contemporary "mass-culture" that "not only influences the young but actually provides the frame within which they sketch their lives." And he is concerned about the question, "what should be the function of the school during a period of cultural debasement?"[11]

But even setting aside the powerful questions asked by Abbs and others,[12] even assuming for a moment that the culture is not wholly "corrupt" and irredeemable in the sense expressed above, the relationship between the contemporary milieu and the Jewish texts that we teach is still problematic for the educator.

Michael Rosenak has aptly described this as the conflict between "authenticity" and "relevance":

> The pristine character of Jewish tradition—demand for technical mastery; alien normative requirements and understandings of knowledge; a religious view of the world which assumes the authority of the Torah and the sovereignty of God; a comprehensive and largely legal character—makes it inaccessible to most pupils, and creates philosophical and other difficulties for many teachers.[13]

Rosenak responds to this difficulty by pointing out that the teacher who argues only on behalf of the authenticity of the tradition (that is, the subject matter) may be working with an overly limited notion of authenticity: that teacher's "basic mistake is that he thinks that only subject matter is authentic. . . . What about the pupils? Don't they have any authenticity?"[14] "An educator," Rosenak concludes,

> has to strive to transmit an authentic teaching and his instruction must make some connection with what children can understand and wish to learn. But if the teacher wages a war on behalf of the subject matter against the pupils, the sincere pupils will be hostile and the simply well-adjusted will be apathetic.[15]

Rosenak presents the question of authenticity and relevance from a Schwabian perspective, though he emphasizes only two of Schwab's four commonplaces. The dangers of subject-matter dominance (that is, pure authenticity) are allayed by the power of the learner's perspective (that is, the need for relevance). Similarly, Rosenak warns, the teacher who leans too much toward the student and against the subject matter will find that "the bright [student] will resent being captive to a non-teacher and the foolish will think that having a good time is all the wisdom there is."[16] It is this dialectic between subject matter and learner that allows, in Schwab's words, "the curriculum making process . . . to function as a countervailing force"[17] guarding both teacher and learner in the process.[18]

Rosenak solves the educator's problem by creating a balancing act between teacher and student, subject matter and learner. There are, however, other possibilities as well. Another approach might address the problem at the level of subject matter itself. We reinvent the subject matter; we rewrite the text itself, one might say, before it ever gets to the student.

Our larger question of milieu becomes relevant here because, I would argue, oftentimes "rewriting the text" is occasioned by pressures from the general culture and its values—either with or without the teacher's awareness of how that rewriting occurs. Or, to put it another way, Rosenak's work seems rooted in the idea that there is an authentic understanding of the tradition and that the teacher often needs to engage in an act of deliberate, self-aware educational "distortion" or adjusting of that authentic meaning in the interests of a legitimate higher good—that the students shall learn the tradition and eventually come to value it on its own terms.

What I am suggesting takes a different slant: the tradition is rewritten, either consciously or unconsciously, not because of the educationally appropriate pressure of being "relevant" to students but because of the power of the milieu and its influence on the teacher's understanding of the subject matter itself. In what way does this happen?

Three possibilities can be delineated: first, the tradition might be "rewritten" because the teacher believes—as a philosophical position—that there is no "authentic" tradition, that the whole idea of authenticity is misguided. This is a view suggested, for example, in the statement by the literary critic Stanley Fish that "meanings are the property neither of fixed and stable texts nor of free and independent readers but of interpretive communities that are responsible both for the shape of a reader's activities and for the texts those activities produce."[19] Hence, we have Derrida's view as presented in Edward L. Greenstein's study of the way that deconstructionist approaches to text might influence our way of reading the Bible:

> The text, the tissue of traces, does not embody or convey meaning. It is the scene of activity in which the reader inscribes meaning. Meaning, then, is unstable. . . . Reading a text is writing a text, inscribing it with the meaning that we find in it.[20]

As Greenstein observes, "The implications for reading biblical narrative can reach as far as one will let them"[21]

Here we find ourselves at the heart of the contemporary debate about postmodern hermeneutics, and it is not necessary in this context to rehearse the complex arguments—from Stanley Fish to E. D. Hirsch with many others in between—on the question of the nature of texts and their readers.[22] But the implications for education in the approach suggested above are clear: the teacher belongs to an interpretive community that understands these texts in a specific, particular way (or ways). The "authentic reading," the *peshat*, if you will, is irrelevant because there is no *peshat!* To put this in traditional Jewish language, one might say that the *torah shebikhtav,* the written Torah, exists only insofar as it is understood by a contemporary *torah sheb'al peh,* an oral Torah. Meanings are always in flux—across time and even across contemporary communities. Thus, my understanding of a Torah passage is as valid as Rabbi Akiva's—in fact, more so, as is suggested by the famous talmudic passage about Moses sitting confused in the *beit midrash* of Akiva.[23] And the readings in my community are as "authentic" as those crafted in Meah Shearim and vice versa.

The position that texts have no inherent "authentic" meanings is one found more commonly in academia and in literary theory than it is in real-life Jewish educational settings, certainly below the university level. More common is a second possibility: the teacher is unaware that what he or she is doing is "rewriting the tradition"—in his or her mind, this *is* the tradition. Rewriting the tradition is essentially midrashic reading, and few would disagree, I believe, that this mode of relationship to the traditional sources has been the dominant approach throughout Jewish history until modernity.[24] The midrashic mode of reading is so powerful and brings with it such an inner consistency that a scholar as rooted in the scientific and academic approach as Gershom Scholem once remarked that when looking at the Zohar's mystical midrash, "even the critical reader is occasionally plagued by doubts whether the true interpretation of certain passages in the Torah may not after all be found here and nowhere else!"[25]

What we know very little about, however, is how the teachers of the past—the rabbis—viewed what they were doing. To say that all the oral Torah was revealed at Sinai is to suggest that the rabbis had very little awareness of their own creative rereadings. On the other hand, to applaud inventive readings, as they did, is to suggest a high degree of reflectiveness about their enterprise.[26] Where the rabbis stood on this issue (and clearly, there is unlikely to be one single position on this matter) is obviously a complex question that deserves much study.

What can be said, however, is that with modernity a great deal changed. Consider the following: a few paragraphs above, I used words like *peshat* and referred to texts such as the Akiva passage in ways that have nothing to do with what are the typical "authentic" understandings of these matters. Now, my own use of these references is self-conscious. I am aware of what I am doing when I am doing it. In that sense, I may be different from my ancestors. Then again, perhaps I am not. At a certain point, even a self-reflective reader (or writer) begins to lose track. What is contemporary manipulation of traditional sources? When does the process become what David Roskies has called "creative betrayal," "the artful fashioning of a new tradition,"[27] and when is it so "natural" that I don't know any longer that I am even doing it?

Thus, the third possibility of my three modes of reading is self-conscious rereading of the past. In some cases, this leads to new interpretations of traditional sources. Perhaps the most obvious example of this kind of self-conscious rereading is the phenomenon of "modern midrash," a lively Jewish literary genre that has flourished in recent years. There are numerous examples of such explorations, ranging from the use of biblical themes, motifs, and language in contemporary Israeli poetry to rereadings of Scripture in the light of contemporary political or social concerns.[28] There is even a new magazine devoted to publishing examples![29]

One striking example of contemporary rereading is the growth of a body of feminist criticism and midrashic writing that examines the classical Jewish canon in the light of women's concerns and consciousness. The feminist literature is varied and wide-ranging in its approaches and interests. Some works apply the methods of academic scholarship to investigate the Bible or the canon of rabbinic literature, asking questions that may not have been asked by researchers in the past because of biases or blind spots about the concerns of women. Others attempt to critique the "patriarchal" orientation of classic Jewish sources. Still others attempt to write new midrashim that are more sensitive to the female characters in the Bible or Talmud or that attempt to reexamine these classic texts in the light of our contemporary concerns.[30]

The reexamination of the classic texts does not always lead to new and reinvigorated readings of old texts. Some feminist critics reject biblical texts as essentially "irredeemable." And such radical critiques are not limited to feminist readers. Particularly in the area of liturgy—

where the words of the prayer book literally become our own spoken words—there are times that certain phrases or ideas become so unacceptable that the text itself is changed. No longer rereading, here we have literal rewriting![31] Thus, although I have been talking above about the power of rereading, in modern times we also find examples that take exactly the opposite route, rejecting the traditional sources either in whole or in part.

There is no more illuminating example of such a radical rejection of traditional texts than the way that the concept of the chosen people was addressed in the thought—and later, the liturgical practice—of one of the most influential Jewish thinkers of the twentieth century, Mordecai M. Kaplan.

Kaplan's ideas about this issue need to be viewed in the context of the challenges that the traditional Jewish doctrine of the chosen people presented to American Jewish leadership—particularly rabbinic leadership—in the twentieth century. Arnold Eisen's study of this topic shows the complexity of the issues faced by these leaders.[32] One core strategy adopted by a number of rabbinic figures, Eisen shows, was a thoroughgoing rereading of the concept of chosenness as mission—that is, being "chosen" does not mean that the Jewish people is better than other people, but that it has a specific obligation, a mission to perform. Here the old language was retained, but its meaning was reinvented. Yet, as Eisen writes, "why did they continue to talk about it—rabbis (and perhaps their congregants) retaining mission and chosenness as the centerpiece of the 'broken myth' they did construct, 'broken' in that its postulates had been denied?"[33]

One dominant American Jewish thinker—in Eisen's words, "the period's most influential, prolific, and incisive Jewish thinker"[34]—however, did not "continue to talk about it":

> Turn where one would . . . one found Mordecai Kaplan with a critique of the traditional idea of election as he understood it, or of one of its many outfittings in modern dress. Turn the election idea as one would, so that a more pleasing side of it faced the modern audience, and Kaplan was there to brush away the cosmetic and show that even in this aspect the idea just could not be countenanced. . . . Chosenness, he insisted, unlike the rest of the Jewish tradition, could not be "reconstructed," but only repudiated.[35]

For Kaplan, "chosenness" was unacceptable for reasons of strategy, politics, ethics, and rational belief. "Reconstructionism [Kaplan's new Jewish ideology] was explicitly meant to replace chosenness, both as the source of pride in Jewish identity and as the purpose for which the Jewish people actively worked."[36]

We might have expected Kaplan to reinterpret the idea of chosenness, as he had many other traditional Jewish concepts. But in one of his major works, *The Meaning of God in Modern Jewish Religion,* Kaplan

> devoted a long section to the enumeration and refutation of all possible reinterpretations of the doctrine of election. Racial theories were groundless. Other peoples had made equal or greater contributions to the world. To say that Israel possessed the highest religious truths was impossible, for truth was a "dynamic concept," ever changing. Finally, election should not be confused with mission. . . . Reinterpretation of election was thus not viable, and the traditional aversion could only be, "ideologically, a definite hindrance."[37]

Why Kaplan believed that the concept of chosenness was "not viable" is related to his own particular conception of Judaism and the nature of Jewish life in America in the first decades of the twentieth century. These issues are not our concern here, and scholars have explored them elsewhere.[38] What is germane to our discussion is the case of Mordecai Kaplan as an example in which "rewriting" does not work, and for whatever historical or personal reasons, even more radical steps were seen to be required.

We have looked at four possible modes of encountering traditional texts—three examples of rereading and one demurral. Kaplan, obviously, is the demurral. In the case of the chosenness of Israel, at least, rewriting is rejected; in other cases, Kaplan developed his own rereading of tradition.

Our three examples of rereading began with those who reject out of hand the notion of any particular "authentic" meaning for any given texts. Written works require interpreters, and interpreters bear the burden of the text's meaning. From there, we moved to a discussion of two less radical approaches to the meaning of texts. The problem of Milieu/capital *M* (the general culture) with which we began relates most directly to the last two modes of reading and teaching: the *unknowing* interpreter in one instance and the *deliberate* midrash-maker in the other. But in either case—whether one is self-conscious about what one is doing or not—the pressures of the general culture will influence one's teaching and present challenges that make teaching Jewish texts in the world of contemporary life difficult indeed. Let us look at three examples of these conflicts, though there are many others that could illustrate the same thesis.

The first example comes from a landmark work of contemporary American sociology. *Habits of the Heart* explores the movement toward individualism that in the authors' view characterizes one of the directions apparent in contemporary American life and religion. As an example, the authors memorably describe one of their interviewees, a young woman named (it is a pseudonym) Sheila Larson:

> Today religion in America is as private and diverse as New England colonial religion was public and unified. One person we interviewed has actually named her religion (she calls it her "faith") after herself. This suggests the logical possibility of over 220 million American religions, one for each of us. . . . [She] describes her faith as "Sheilaism." "I believe in God. I'm not a religious fanatic. I can't remember the last time I went to church. My faith has carried me a long way. It's Sheilaism. Just my own little voice." . . . In defining "my own Sheilaism," she said: "It's just try to love yourself and be gentle with yourself. You know, I guess, take care of each other. I think He would want us to take care of each other."[39]

What are the characteristics of Sheila's religious faith? First, it is interesting to note that hers is a "moderate," *theistic* religion. She believes in God, and she distances herself from a kind of religious fanaticism that *Habits of the Heart* elsewhere sees as prevalent in some elements of American culture in our times. The strikingly high quotient of "belief in God" among Americans as revealed regularly in social science research seems once again to be confirmed in this case.[40] But belief in God is only one aspect of a religious worldview and culture. As we can see, Sheilaism is a religion that has virtually no public expressions of faith (she hasn't been to church in a very long time) and demands of practice. It is a kind of Protestantism taken to a parodic endpoint—there are no "works" at all (no mitzvot, Jews would say), no worship, no moral code beyond loving oneself and "I guess"(!) taking care of others.

Second, this is a highly individualized religion—symbolized, of course, by her naming the religion after herself! The individualism appears to flow directly out of tenets of her "faith": a religion with virtually no demands easily becomes a version of narcissism. Although it is likely that a position as radical as Sheila's does not represent a broad crosscurrent of contemporary American religious belief, it is also probable that the two elements of an internalized religious faith without demands of public expression and a highly individualized religious perspective represent very deep currents within the religious consciousness of many Americans today.

We may see this even more clearly when we turn to one of the dominant voices of contemporary culture—at least, as it is experienced by children: the animated films of Walt Disney Productions. In Disney's recent works, it is not difficult to discern versions of ideas related to those expressed by Sheila, though couched in a far less radical language. Disney's 1994 production *The Lion King* tells the story of a young African lion, Simba, whose father, Mufasa, the king of the lions, is killed by an evil plot engineered by the king's brother. Convinced that he himself was to blame, Simba leaves the lion pride and goes into exile. Eventually, bolstered by the new friends that he has made, by the reappearance of the love of his youth, and mostly by his sense of princely responsibility, he returns to the Prideland, overthrows his hated uncle (who has in the meanwhile settled down with Simba's mother), and takes his place as the rightful king.

The Lion King is a successful and effective cinematic experience for children. (One need only look at its immense popularity and astronomical sales.) At once drawing on Disney's vaunted animation skills, the power of folk motifs (the succession of kings, the prince in exile, the evil uncle), and a lively musical score, it is no wonder that the film has been such a hit. In addition, it is not far-fetched to think of *The Lion King* as a version of yet another long-popular drama, Shakespeare's *Hamlet,* albeit in this case *Hamlet* with a happy ending! The murdered king, the indecisive son racked with guilt, the mother who marries the murderer—these are familiar elements to audiences from at least the early seventeenth century.

But Disney's *Lion King* adds other things as well, and these may also play a role in its success and popularity. Its Shakespearean and folk motifs are mixed with versions of the contemporary American religious ethos that we began exploring earlier, elements far removed from *Hamlet* or fairy tales.

Early in the movie, Mufasa tells Simba that someday he, the king, will die and Simba will succeed him. He begins to explain to his son the power and limitations of being a king:

Simba: But I thought a king can do whatever he wants.

Mufasa: There's more to being king than getting your way every time.

Simba: There's more?

Mufasa: Simba! Everything you see exists together in a delicate balance. As king you need to understand that balance and respect all the creatures, from the crawling ant to the leaping antelope.

Simba: But don't we eat the antelopes?

Mufasa: Yes, Simba, but let me explain it to you: When we die, our bodies become the grass and the antelopes eat the grass. We are all connected in the great circle of life.[41]

Years later, after Mufasa has died and Simba has run away, Simba experiences a mysterious encounter in which he hears his father urging him to return home and take his rightful place as king. "You have forgotten who you are," says the ghostly voice (*Hamlet* again!). "Look inside yourself, Simba. You are more than you have become. You must take your place in the circle of life. Remember who you are."[42]

One of the powerful messages of the film is a kind of religious ecological spirit that permeates its consciousness: we are all connected in the circle of life. The movie is careful to avoid any specifically theistic images. Now, the producers of the film are not theologians. They are in the business of making money from movies. The specific choices made here are no doubt strongly motivated by commercial considerations— Disney's desire to appeal to the greatest numbers and offend the fewest. But for that very reason, we should not underestimate the skill with which these moviemakers have gauged the reigning pulse of the American spirit. It is not accidental that the movie *The Lion King*, on film and on video, has been one of the largest moneymakers in movie history.

Another, slightly later, Disney film also deals with these issues. *Pocahontas*[43] makes the ecological spirit of *The Lion King* even more dominant. Retelling the legend of the Indian princess Pocahontas, the movie is working out a number of different agendas. One is an exploration of the nature of what it means to be "civilized." The movie presents the life of the native American "savages" as the truly advanced society; the white conquerors are the real savages, incapable of understanding the beauty of the world they are entering until the Indian princess teaches them.

The native Indians live in harmony with their environment, and that harmony is related to a rich nature religion that comes up a number of times in the film. In Pocahontas herself and even more dramatically in the character of Grandmother Willow, a talking tree who represents the wisdom and core values promulgated by the film, the message of a spiritualized nature is expressed. Early in the movie, Grandmother Willow gives advice to Pocahontas:

Pocahontas: Grandmother Willow, what is my path? How am I ever going to find it?

Grandmother Willow: Your mother asked me the very same question.

Pocahontas: She did? What did you tell her?

GW: I told her to listen. All around you, child, are spirits. They live in the earth, the water, the sky. If you listen, they will guide you.

Pocahontas: I hear the wind.

GW: Yes, what is it telling you?

Pocahontas: I don't understand.

GW: . . . Listen with your heart. You will understand.[44]

Later, Grandmother Willow will urge Pocahontas to "let the spirits of the earth guide you,"[45] as Pocahontas seeks to find her "path." Pocahontas teaches John Smith and the rest of the settlers two fundamental messages, summed up in the movie's big song, "Colors of the Wind." One teaching is about universal brotherhood and the evils of racism. (She sings to Smith: "You think the only people who are people are the people who look and think like you.") The other lesson is summed up in the following verses:

> Pocahontas (sings): You think you own whatever earth you land
> on. The earth is just a dead thing you can
> claim.
> But I know every rock and tree and creature
> Has a life, has a spirit, has a name.
>
> The rainstorm and the river are my brothers.
> The heron and the otter are my friends.
> We are all connected to each other
> In a circle, in a hoop, that never ends.[46]

As in *The Lion King,* the "circle" of life reappears here as well. (Note the addition here of the word "hoop" from Native American culture.)

What happens when we see the way these ideas play themselves out in the Jewish realm? In an essay entitled "Judaism for the Post-Modern Era,"[47] Arthur Green, a contemporary scholar and theologian, explored this issue by analyzing an advertisement placed in the "Personals" column of New York's *Jewish Week* newspaper not too long ago. The notice had been posted by a 34-year-old divorced Jewish woman seeking a Jewish mate. What Green focused on was her description of herself as "spiritual not religious." What might that mean, he asked, and in what way was she emblematic of other Jews? In what way was she, as he puts it, "an icon of our age"?[48] He goes on to imagine what this "spiritual not religious" person might be like. Among the many insights that emerge from Green's imaginative exercise is the following reflection:

> She doesn't know whether she believes in God. Certainly the God-centered religion she encountered in the synagogue never spoke much to her. . . .

> But this agnosticism is of a new sort. It emphatically is not about a denial of spirituality. . . . For her, spirituality is something that begins from within, has to do with a perception of the universe, with a perspective on existence itself. . . . It is a sense that all of being is One, that each of us is an expression of an inner core of Oneness. . . . If there is something she could call *God* it is that inner Oneness. But she'd just as soon call it *universal soul* or

breath as some of the Yoga teachers do. . . . But all this does not mean that there is someone she wants to *worship*.[49]

Green's analysis in this essay leads to an argument advocating the need to make available to such seekers the resources of Judaism's own rich spiritual tradition, in particular the teachings of Jewish mysticism. But, he is careful to point out, this is not an easy task. Seekers such as the woman in the ad are not likely to end up embracing traditional Jewish practice or mainstream theology. Reimagining Jewish theology for contemporary times and anchoring it at the same time in classical Jewish conceptions of God—albeit ideas that emanate from the Jewish spiritual tradition—would be a major undertaking. Do we have the will, the resources, and the thinkers who can invent such versions of Jewish theology—at once radically different from what most Jews have learned and at the same time rooted in the classical sources of the tradition?

And there are other challenges as well. The issues of Jewish "competency" and the inaccessibility of many classic Jewish sources cannot easily be divorced from any such discussion. In a later essay that expands on some of the same themes, Green points out:

> Judaism is a highly verbal tradition, and its language is Hebrew. Nobody says that you have to learn Pali or Tibetan or Japanese to be a good Buddhist. . . .
>
> [But] to do the Jewish spiritual life seriously, you really do have to know Hebrew. Our prayer traditions are highly verbal and tied to the intricacies of language, so that they just don't work in translation. So much of our teaching, including the deepest insights of the mystical and Hasidic sources, is caught up in plays and nuances of language that translation of such sources, while it is to be increased and encouraged, will never quite be adequate.[50]

Without access to Hebrew, without the basic skills that define a person's ability to participate in a religious Jewish community—how to say the blessing, when to sit and stand, where to face at certain times in prayer—it is hard indeed to make sense of the liturgy or gain easy access to Jewish communal life.

And finally, there is the question of the fit between the contemporary seeker's views and the worldview of the tradition called Judaism. Green asks the following question:

> How do we reply to the Jewish seeker who says: "Yes, I am a religious person. I believe in the oneness of all being. I feel a connection to something eternal and infinite that is present in my own soul and in yours. That's what my quest is all about. But I can't call it 'God'"?[51]

For people living in the world of contemporary America, the world of Disney's Pocahontas, such statements are perfectly in harmony with the spiritual message of the times. But, as Green says, "even the most spiritualized form of Judaism is focused on knowing, loving, and obeying God in one way or another. Is it in any way conceivable that one seeks to have a *Jewish* spiritual life without 'believing in God'?"[52]

These three examples indicate key difficulties for the teaching of Jewish texts in our time. We have spoken about the challenges to Jewish education presented by contemporary American culture. In what ways do Jewish tradition and the classic Jewish texts differ from the worldview that we have been exploring? Let us look at five elements that are generally characteristic of Jewish religious consciousness throughout most of its history to see the nature of these conflicts.

To begin with, Jewish traditional sources reflect a theistic conception of the world. The texts assume that there is a God and that that God is deeply connected to the events of our world. Although it is certainly true that Jewish conceptions of God are far more varied and complex than many Jews realize—that, for example, the God of Maimonides, the God of Akiva, the God of the Zohar, and the God of Deuteronomy are remarkably different each from the next—the assertion that there is a God who is involved with humanity is virtually universal in Jewish sources, at least until modern times. Even in cases in which theology verged on the pantheistic, such as in certain versions of Hasidism,[53] it is still far away indeed from the animistic "spirits of the earth" of Pocahontas.

Second, the classic texts affirm the existence of a set of divinely ordained rules by which human beings are to conduct their lives. These rules—given by God and interpreted, perhaps embellished, by people—are the mitzvot, the commandments, which are present in virtually every human activity. Although these rules may have a certain rational logic (and this is a matter of debate among the sources), the ultimate reason for doing them is that they are commandments from God and agreed to by Israel at the covenant of Sinai.[54] Thus, the commandments at their source are not based on reason. These are not "any old rules": these are God's commandments. Human ingenuity may discover many good reasons for doing them, but the power of doing them does not emanate from our interpretations. Nor are the commandments relativistic, that is, we do not speak about the "Ten Suggestions," but the "Ten Commandments."[55] And the rules themselves are eternally relevant and applicable.

The fact that the commandments are not relativistic leads to a third dimension of this worldview. Namely, the classical sources share a _particularistic_ consciousness about the world. This particularism manifests itself in two ways. One is the notion that Israel has a special relationship with God and a special place in God's world. The commandments are demanding, true, but they also represent a higher level of relationship to God. Indeed, it is probably true that until modernity, most Jews thought of Israel's religion as *better* than the religions of others. And even today, many Jews may harbor the secret, unspoken idea, "Jews are better."[56] The other way is that, even where Jewish texts express "universalistic" values, the primary focus of those texts still remains on Israel and its particular situation vis-à-vis those values.

Fourth, the classic Jewish consciousness views Torah as the ultimate source of wisdom. In a certain sense, this is yet another aspect of particularism, but I would suggest that it goes beyond that. It is a kind of exclusivism about the nature of truth. At times, this understanding of Torah means denying that any wisdom is to be found in the teachings of the rest of the world. But even where texts admit or accept the possibility that truth might be found elsewhere as well, it is generally with the understanding that these other truths are either subservient to Torah (such as with technical or practical knowledge—medicine, for example) or that these ideas are also to be found in Israel's Torah.[57]

Finally, Jewish tradition is powerfully oriented toward the community rather than the individual. This is both an ideological position and a datum of history and sociology. In the latter case, of course, Jews spent most of their history living as a minority in an often hostile or barely tolerant majority culture. Emphasis on community rather than the individual strengthened and preserved a minority culture. Even in the contemporary State of Israel, the power of community values has been at the core of most of its history.[58] The sociological realities worked in symbiosis with an ideological emphasis on community, and it is impossible to say which influenced which. Certainly in this realm, there was room for individual expression, individual prayer, and meditation, for example. But by and large, communal values—whether it be the first-person-plural language of most prayers or the need for a minyan to say the Kaddish—tended to overrule the other.

God, nonrelativistic rules of behavior, particularism, the ultimate, often exclusivistic understanding of the wisdom of Torah, and the communal orientation—these are powerful elements of the classical tradition. Where is "Sheilaism" or Disney universalism?

What does it mean to teach a communal tradition in a culture that lauds individualism? What does it mean to teach a tradition with explicit demands on behavior in a culture that resents anyone telling anyone else what to do? What does it mean to teach a tradition with specific religious and theological content in a culture that values a kind of free-floating spirituality?

Most importantly, for those who value and want to live in the general culture—that is, the vast majority of Jews in America—the power of that culture's "common religion" is extremely well rooted and pronounced. Teaching Jewish texts means swimming against a powerful and long-standing current.

Where does this all come from, and why is it so powerful? One can, of course, find many sources, but here I would like to point toward the roots of our American "religious" or pseudo-religious culture today as emanating from one dominating figure—Ralph Waldo Emerson. Emersonian religion, particularly as found in his great early work *Nature*, though controversial in his own time to be sure, has become *the* American religion at the turn of our millennium, and trying to dislodge roots so well established is no mean task.

Emerson's *Nature*, in the words of the important recent study by Robert D. Richardson, Jr., "asserted a new conception of religion as a phenomenon that manifested itself more fully through nature, especially human nature, than through old texts, religious institutions, or reported miracles."[59] Richardson's words point to our difficulties. It is hard to imagine a text more problematic for Judaism than the remarkable opening words of Emerson's small book. It is equally hard to imagine writing that is more emblematic of contemporary American consciousness:

Our age is retrospective. It builds the sepulchres of the fathers. It writes biographies, histories, and criticism. The foregoing generations beheld God and nature face to face; we, through their eyes. Why should not we also enjoy an original relation to the universe? Why should not we have a poetry and philosophy of insight and not of tradition, and a religion by revelation to us, and not the history of theirs? . . . [W]hy should we grope among the dry bones of the past or put the living generation into masquerade out of its faded wardrobe? The sun shines to-day also. There is more wool and flax in the fields. There are new lands, new men, new thoughts. Let us demand our own works and laws and worship.[60]

Emerson begins by commenting on the natural human tendency to look to the past for wisdom. Our ancestors had *real* religious experiences—they "beheld God and nature face to face." We, on the other hand, only know God "through their eyes." Then suddenly, there is a shift. As if struck by a surprising new idea, Emerson asks, what about us? "Why should not we also enjoy an original relation to the universe?" From that moment on, the past is set aside. Tradition is not what we need, he says. Rather, "let us demand our own works and laws and worship."

This demand—to reject the past and create a new religious life in the present—is not the only aspect of Emerson that speaks to the religious consciousness we see around us today. Equally powerful is his evocation of nature itself, as religious experience:

In the woods, we return to reason and faith. There I feel that nothing can befall me in life,—no disgrace, no calamity, (leaving me my eyes,) which nature cannot repair. Standing on the bare ground,—my head bathed by the blithe air, and uplifted into infinite space,—all mean egotism vanishes. I become a transparent eye-ball; I am nothing; I see all; the currents of the Universal Being circulate through me; I am part or particle of God. The name of the nearest friend sounds then foreign and accidental: to be brothers, to be acquaintances,—master or servant, is then a trifle and a disturbance.[61]

Here we have a combination of a kind of nature mysticism and individualism. Once one has experienced being "part or particle of God" in nature, the need for community ("to be brothers") disappears. At one with the spirit of the American woods, we might say, there is no need for a minyan or *kehilla*.

Emerson's religious message encompasses two dimensions that we have seen in the passage from *Nature*—the mystical merging with "Universal Being" and the individual who stands alone in his or her religious faith. Individualism lurks behind this passage and inhabits a special place in much of Emerson's writing. It is expressed directly in the most well known of all his essays, "Self-Reliance."

"Trust thyself," says Emerson, "every heart vibrates to that iron string."[62] Emerson in this essay rails against the dangers of conformity, consistency, and an unhealthy concern for the opinion of others. "Society," he warns, "everywhere is in conspiracy against the manhood of every one of its members. . . . Whoso would be a man, must be a nonconformist. . . . Nothing is at last sacred but the integrity of our own mind."[63]

What about law, one might ask, what about divine commands? Emerson rejects it: "What have I to do with the sacredness of traditions, if I live wholly from within? . . . No law can be sacred to me but that of my nature. Good and bad are but names very readily transferable to that or this; the only right is what is after my constitution, the only wrong what is against it."[64]

If not law, then, what about a sense of personal duty, what about obligations to others around you? Emerson answers:

[D]o not tell me, as a good man did to-day, of my obligation to put all poor men in good situations. Are they *my* poor? I tell thee, thou foolish philanthropist, that I grudge the dollar, the dime, the cent I give to such men as do not belong to me and to whom I do not belong. . . . [B]ut your miscellaneous popular charities; the education at college of fools; the building of meeting-houses to the vain end to which many now stand; alms to sots; and the thousandfold Relief Societies;—though I confess with shame I sometimes succumb and give the dollar, it is a wicked dollar which by and by I shall have the manhood to withhold.[65]

The Emerson of "Self-Reliance" expresses ideals that deeply inform American religious (and popular) consciousness. They are ideas that live far from the social realities of the classic Jewish community—with its emphasis on *externally* determined law (that is, mitzvot and halakhah)—and with its rich sense of the individual's necessary obligations to his or her community. Contrast for a moment the quotation from

Emerson above about resisting demands to contribute to charity with Maimonides' famous statements about the levels of *tzedakah*.[66] Nothing would seem "less Jewish" than Emerson's advice. Unless perhaps this: "When we have broken our god of tradition," Emerson says in "The Over-Soul," "and ceased from our god of rhetoric, then may God fire the heart with his presence."[67] To experience God, then, we must forget about communal strictures, laws, and practices. We must set aside the words of texts—"rhetoric," as he puts it here—and leave all "tradition" behind.

The leap between the sophisticated Platonic idealism of Emerson and the pop rhythms of Disney's *Pocahontas* or the Personals column in a newspaper may seem great indeed, but in many ways what we are witnessing in our own time is the popularized, perhaps bastardized, version of a deep religious consciousness strongly rooted in the American soil. The native Americans encountered by John Smith in the Disney movie are natural mystics. Their trees literally speak wisdom. Emerson may be the most powerful expression of this American religious perspective, but its sources go back a long time, and it is no wonder that we find its influences around us in a variety of ways. Perry Miller, the influential American intellectual historian, in his famous essay "From Edwards to Emerson,"[68] tried to show ways in which this perspective reached back to the Puritan beginnings on the continent—back, one might say, almost to the time of Pocahontas.[69]

Miller suggested that one could see the roots of Emersonian mysticism in the greatest of the American Puritan thinkers, Jonathan Edwards (1703–58). Edwards himself, argued Miller, differed from those who came before him—Edwards had "discovered a different cosmos from that of the seventeenth century, a dynamic world, filled with the presence of God, quickened with divine life, pervaded with joy and ecstasy."[70] But what is consistent from the "covenant theology" of the early Puritans to Edwards and through to Emerson was "the Puritan's effort to confront, face to face, the image of a blinding divinity in the physical universe, and to look up that universe without the intermediacy of ritual, of ceremony, of the Mass and the confessional."[71]

Puritanism, in Miller's view, was characterized by two competing impulses. One was the tendency toward a mystical, unmediated experience of God; the other was a tightly knit communal structure with authoritative—one might say authoritarian—rules. This latter dimension is closer to what our popular notion of the word "Puritan" means. (Indeed, the image of Puritan social control and strictness goes back at least to Nathaniel Hawthorne's story "The Maypole of Merrymount" [1836].)

Miller argued that by Emerson's time, the second part of the Puritan *paedeia*—self-control and decorum—had been appropriated into the culture of "good" society. It had been transformed into good manners and bourgeois social conventions. But, he asked, "what of the mysticism, the hunger of the soul, the sense of divine emanation in man and in nature, which had been so important an element in the Puritan character? Had it died out in New England?"[72] The answer was a resounding no! Emerson's *Nature* was a powerful continuation of that tradition—though it used a language and terms of reference far different from what had gone before.

Thus, the roots of our contemporary culture's religious consciousness run very deep. According to Miller's view, they go back 300 years, and, at the very least, Emersonian religion has been in the air for 150 years. For Jewish education, these are indeed powerful dimensions of the milieu in which we practice our craft.

So how do we deal with the problem of milieu? Clearly, we can't fight it by isolating ourselves. We teach students who live in the context of contemporary culture, who watch television, listen to music, and spend a great deal of time absorbing the products of the "media."

We do need to be aware of what the challenges are—looking carefully at the culture around us, considering ways that teaching texts like the Bible is both a challenge for our students and—in a more positive way—an antidote to some of the weaknesses in the culture in which they live. For in the ways that the contemporary milieu is shallow, the Bible is profound; in the ways that the contemporary milieu is manipulated, "spun," and "branded," the Bible casts a cold eye on human frailty and forces us to face ourselves head-on.

Most of all for those of us who are educators, we need to deal with this by teaching better! What would that mean? Certainly, we need a clearer sense of goals—we need to understand what lies behind our teaching, and we need to articulate better *why* we are doing what we are doing.

How does the study of Bible encounter the Emersonian universe, and how does our reading and rereading of texts help our students make sense both of that world and the tradition from which we have come? This is our challenge, and it will require our best thinking and most inventive approaches to pedagogy if we are to succeed in the

Emersonian world that we all inhabit. In the next chapter, we will begin our exploration by considering ways that our pedagogic goals and our knowledge of the Bible are bound up more closely with each other than we might have realized. What does it mean for a teacher to "know" the subject matter that he or she is teaching? In what ways might teachers "hold" that knowledge? How is that knowledge linked to our pedagogic goals? We will turn to these questions now.

Notes

1. Allen Grossman, "Teaching Literature in a Discredited Civilization: A Talk for Teachers," *The Massachusetts Review* (summer 1969): 419–32.
2. Lawrence A. Cremin, *Public Education* (New York: Basic Books, 1976).
3. Ralph W. Tyler, *Basic Principles of Curriculum and Instruction* (Chicago: University of Chicago Press, 1949), pp. 16ff.
4. Commonplaces, according to Schwab, are "those foci of attention within an area of interest which fulfill two conditions: a) They demand the attention of serious investigators; b) their scrutiny generates diverse investigations and consequent diversities of definitions, doctrines, and emphases." Joseph Schwab, "Problems, Topics, and Issues," in *Education and the Structure of Knowledge,* ed. Stanley Elam (Chicago: Rand, McNally, 1964), pp. 5–6.
5. Joseph J. Schwab, "The Practical 3: Translation into Curriculum" (1973), in idem, *Science, Curriculum, and Liberal Education,* ed. Ian Westbury and Neil J. Wilkof (Chicago: University of Chicago Press, 1978), p. 366.
6. Ibid., p. 367.
7. Seymour Fox, "The Vitality of Theory in Schwab's Conception of the Practical," *Curriculum Inquiry* 15, no. 1 (1985): 76.
8. Ibid.
9. Samuel C. Heilman, *Defenders of the Faith* (New York: Schocken, 1992).
10. For one aspect of this worldview, see the discussion of the ultraorthodox concept of "exile within the land of Israel," in Aviezer Ravitzky, *Messianism, Zionism and Jewish Religious Radicalism* (Chicago: University of Chicago Press, 1993), pp. 145–55.
11. Peter Abbs, *Reclamations* (London: Heinemann, 1979), p. 54.
12. For example, Neil Postman, *Amusing Ourselves to Death: Public Discourse in the Age of Show Business* (New York: Viking, 1985).
13. Michael Rosenak, *Teaching Jewish Values: A Conceptual Guide* (Jerusalem: Melton Centre for Jewish Education in the Diaspora, 1986), p. 37.
14. Ibid., p. 46.
15. Ibid., p. 53.
16. Ibid.

17. Schwab, "The Practical 3," p. 368.
18. For more on the this process, see Fox, "The Vitality of Theory," pp. 72–73.
19. Stanley Fish, "How to Recognize a Poem When You See One," in his *Is There a Text in This Class?* (Cambridge: Harvard University Press, 1980), p. 322.
20. Edward L. Greenstein, "Deconstruction and Biblical Narrative," in *Interpreting Judaism in a Postmodern Age,* ed. Steven Kepnes (New York: New York University Press, 1996), p. 31.
21. Ibid.
22. There are a number of excellent analyses exploring the issue of contemporary literary interpretation. Among them: William E. Cain, *The Crisis in Criticism* (Baltimore: Johns Hopkins University Press, 1984); Robert Scholes, *Protocols of Reading* (New Haven: Yale University Press, 1989); Terry Eagleton, *Literary Theory: An Introduction,* 2d ed. (Oxford: Blackwell, 1996); and K. M. Newton, *Interpreting the Text* (New York and London: Harvester Wheatsheaf, 1990).
23. Babylonian Talmud, Menahot 29b.
24. See introduction to my *Back to the Sources: Reading the Classic Jewish Texts* (New York: Summit / Simon and Schuster, 1984).
25. Gershom Scholem, *Major Trends in Jewish Mysticism* (New York: Schocken, 1961), p. 158. Scholem is actually paraphrasing David Neumark. My thanks to Professor Arthur Green for pointing this reference out to me.
26. See my discussion of this issue in *Back to the Sources,* pp. 13–16.
27. David Roskies, *A Bridge of Longing: The Lost Art of Yiddish Storytelling* (Cambridge: Harvard University Press, 1995), pp. 4–5.
28. See, for example: David Jacobson, *Modern Midrash* (Albany: State University of New York Press, 1987); and Arthur Waskow, *Godwrestling—Round 2* (Woodstock, Vt.: Jewish Lights, 1996).
29. *Living Text,* published in Philadelphia.
30. See the series edited by Athaliah Brenner, *The Feminist Companion to . . .* various books of the Bible (Sheffield, Eng.: Sheffield Academic Press); Mieke Bal, *Lethal Love* (Bloomington: Indiana University Press, 1987), and her *Murder and Difference: Gender, Genre, and Scholarship on Sisera's Death* (Bloomington: Indiana University Press, 1989); Alice Bach, *Women, Seduction and Betrayal in Biblical Narrative* (Cambridge: Cambridge University Press, 1997); Judith A. Kates and Gail Twersky Reimer, *Reading Ruth* (New York: Ballantine, 1994); and Judith Hauptman, *Rereading the Rabbis: A Woman's Voice* (Boulder, Colo.: Westview, 1998).
31. See my discussion in Holtz, *Finding Our Way: Jewish Texts and the Lives We Lead Today* (New York: Schocken, 1990), pp. 110–35.
32. Arnold M. Eisen, *The Chosen People in America: A Study in Jewish Religious Ideology* (Bloomington: Indiana University Press, 1983).
33. Ibid., p. 67.
34. Ibid., p. 73.
35. Ibid.

36. Ibid., p. 76.

37. Ibid., p. 81.

38. Ibid., pp. 93–98. Also Ira Eisenstein, "Kaplan as Liturgist," in *The American Judaism of Mordecai M. Kaplan*, ed. Emanuel S. Goldsmith, Mel Scult, and Robert M. Seltzer (New York: New York University Press, 1990), pp. 319–34; Mel Scult, *Judaism Faces the Twentieth Century: A Biography of Mordecai M. Kaplan* (Detroit: Wayne State University Press, 1993); and Jeffrey S. Gurock and Jacob J. Schacter, *A Modern Heretic and a Traditional Community* (New York: Columbia University Press, 1997).

39. Robert Bellah et al., *Habits of the Heart* (Berkeley: University of California Press, 1985), pp. 220–21.

40. See Barry A. Kosmin and Seymour P. Lachman, *One Nation under God: Religion in Contemporary American Society* (New York: Harmony, 1993).

41. Walt Disney Productions, 1994, at 8 minutes, 50 seconds into the film.

42. Ibid., at 1 hour, 5 minutes, 50 seconds into the film.

43. Walt Disney Productions, 1995.

44. Ibid., at 13 minutes, 55 seconds into the film.

45. Ibid., at 1 hour, 8 minutes, 35 seconds into the film.

46. Ibid., at 38 minutes, 10 seconds into the film.

47. Arthur Green, "Judaism for the Post Modern Era," Samuel H. Goldenson Lecture, Hebrew Union College–Jewish Institute of Religion, Cincinnati, 12 December 1994.

48. Ibid., p. 4.

49. Ibid., pp. 5–6.

50. Arthur Green, "Restoring the Aleph: Judaism for the Contemporary Seeker" (New York: Council for Initiatives in Jewish Education [CIJE], 1996), p. 17.

51. Ibid., p. 19.

52. Ibid., p. 18.

53. See Louis Jacobs, *Seeker of Unity: The Life and Works of Aaron of Starosselje* (London: Vallentine, Mitchell, 1966); and Rachel Elior, *The Paradoxical Ascent to God: The Kabbalistic Theosophy of Habad Hasidim* (Albany: State University of New York Press, 1993).

54. See, for example, the famous passage in Maimonides, *Guide of the Perplexed*, III, 26. See the discussion in Isadore Twersky, *Introduction to the Code of Maimonides [Mishneh Torah]* (New Haven: Yale University Press, 1980), pp. 374–415. I discuss various views on the reasons for the commandments in Holtz, *Finding Our Way*, pp. 39–63.

55. At least, in English; in Hebrew, the expression, interestingly, is *aseret hadibrot*— "the ten utterances."

56. For an informative exploration of this topic, see Joshua Halberstam, *Schmoozing: The Private Conversations of American Jews* (New York: Berkley Publishing Group, A Perigee Book, 1997), pp. 48–73.

57. In the Middle Ages, the tension between the domain of secular knowledge and

its authority, on the one hand, and the wisdom of the tradition, on the other, became a particularly powerful issue. In the words of Isadore Twersky: "In the final analysis two conflicting ideal types were juxtaposed: a traditional puritanism which is distrustful of secular culture and insists on the absolute opposition between divine wisdom and human wisdom; and religious rationalism which is convinced of the interrelatedness and complementarity . . . of divine and human wisdom . . . and strives doggedly for their integration." In his *Maimonides Reader* (New York: Behrman House, 1972), p. 25.

58. See the discussion of this theme in Yaron Ezrahi, *Rubber Bullets* (New York: Farrar, Straus & Giroux, 1997).

59. Robert D. Richardson, Jr., *Emerson: The Mind on Fire* (Berkeley: University of California Press, 1995), p. 225.

60. Ralph Waldo Emerson, *Nature,* in *Essays and Lectures* (New York: Library of America, 1983), p. 7.

61. Ibid., p. 10.

62. Ralph Waldo Emerson, "Self-Reliance," in *Essays and Lectures,* p. 260.

63. Ibid., p. 261.

64. Ibid., p. 262.

65. Ibid., pp. 262–63.

66. *Mishneh Torah,* "Gifts to the Poor," chap. 10, pp. 7–14.

67. Ralph Waldo Emerson, "The Over-Soul," in *Essays and Lectures,* p. 398.

68. Perry Miller, "From Edwards to Emerson," in his *Errand into the Wilderness* (Cambridge: Harvard University Press, 1956), pp. 184–203.

69. For a more recent study, see Catherine L. Albanese, *Nature Religion in America* (Chicago: University of Chicago Press, 1990), and her bibliographical note beginning on p. 239.

70. Miller, "From Edwards to Emerson," p. 195.

71. Ibid., p. 185.

72. Ibid., p. 196.

CHAPTER TWO

The Bible and the Goals
of Jewish Education:
What We Can and Cannot Learn
from General Education

As a teacher, a teacher of the Bible and the Jewish tradition in particular, I spend my time with texts. Texts are the lifeblood of the enterprise, the words we grapple with and argue with, the materials we fashion and refashion, the language we make our own. Sometimes it may be the words of Genesis or the midrashic and medieval commentaries on those tales. At other times, it is the Book of Psalms or the prophetic poetry of Jeremiah. But no matter what the particular text is, as teachers of this tradition, mostly we read and we talk. In doing so, we are forced to look at our purposes, to try to articulate the goals behind the work we do. Often these goals move us simultaneously in two different directions, each demanding allegiance. Consider, by way of example, two very different definitions of education itself. The first, quite short, is by Bernard Bailyn, as quoted by the historian of American education Lawrence Cremin in *Public Education*: "Education is the entire process by which culture transmits itself across the generations."[1]

I've thought about this definition quite a bit over the years, and in many ways it seems very close to the essence of what I am trying to do as a *Jewish* teacher. The activities of Jewish education are deeply involved in the enterprise of cultural transmission. Jewish teachers see themselves, quite legitimately, as heirs and protectors of a great resource. The project of Jewish teaching, from this point of view, is passing on the legacy, the content, and the riches of the Jewish past. And it is a weighty assignment.

Yet, much as I have relied on this presentation of our task, I have been bothered by it as well. My difficulties become clearer when we consider the following alternative definition:

As civilised human beings, we are the inheritors, neither of an inquiry about ourselves and the world, nor of an accumulating
body of information, but of a conversation, begun in the
primeval forests and extended and made more articulate in the
course of centuries. It is a conversation which goes on both in
public and within each of ourselves. Of course there is argument
and inquiry and information, but wherever these are profitable
they are to be recognized as passages in this conversation, and
perhaps they are not the most captivating of the passages. . . .
Conversation is not an enterprise designed to yield an extrinsic
profit, a contest where a winner gets a prize, nor is it an activity
of exegesis; it is an unrehearsed intellectual adventure. . . . Education, properly speaking, is an initiation into the skill and part-
nership of this conversation in which we learn to recognize the
voices, to distinguish the proper occasions of utterance, and in
which we acquire the intellectual and moral habits appropriate
to conversation. And it is this conversation which, in the end,
gives place and character to every human activity and utterance.[2]

The passage is from Michael Oakeshott and is a view profoundly
different from Bailyn's. Education here is not the "transmission" of
anything specific—not "an accumulating body of information," as
Oakeshott puts it—but is instead "initiation" of a very particular sort:
we are to learn the skills and the nature of a "conversation" that goes
back to the beginning of time. What the exact content of the conversation is, Oakeshott does not tell us; though from his language, I believe
we are to understand that it is the basic encounter with the meaning
and significance of human experience itself. He does tell us that it is
"an unrehearsed intellectual adventure" that requires certain competencies, dispositions, and habits. Our task as educators, according to
Oakeshott, is to prepare students who can participate in this great un-
ending conversation.

As a Jewish educator, I am neatly caught between the Scylla of
Oakeshott and the Charybdis of Bailyn. I know that the Jewish tradition encompasses, one might say, a package: of ideas, competencies, attitudes, virtues, and proscribed behaviors. I have inherited that package
from my ancestors, and insofar as I am able to hand it over to others,
particularly to younger generations, I will have succeeded as an educator. And yet on the other hand, I also know that the transmission of culture, Bailyn-like, is only part of our task as Jewish educators. The word

"transmission" is too passive, too unengaged. As educators, we are also involved in the enterprise of new creation, of active "conversation," as Oakeshott would have it. True, we want to nurture students who will receive an inheritance of narratives and laws, but we also want to encourage them to enter that conversation actively, to create new tales, new readings of the law, new interpretations, new ways of understanding the old.

In describing this dilemma, I do not believe that I am creating some kind of straw-man dichotomy between the Bailyn view and the Oakeshott view, something unrelated to the living realities of teachers and students. For it is worthwhile to remember that lurking behind all that we do as teachers is a kind of enemy, a shadow that darkens every teacher's class: namely, the specter of time. Better yet, the time we do *not* have: so many texts, so little time. Therefore, the choices we make matter; we do not have world enough and time; we have our students only briefly no matter what the educational context, and, it goes without saying, we are confronted by the fact that though time is short, the Jewish tradition is very big. Thus, any particular focus that we choose in our teaching needs to be well thought out and clearly expressive of the ultimate aims that matter most to us in our work.

This conflict, essentially a struggle between worthy, but competing, educational aims, is similar to that described by Philip Jackson as two "traditions" of "distinguishably different ways of thinking about education and of translating that thought into practice."[3] Jackson calls these the "mimetic" tradition and the "transformative" tradition. In one—the mimetic—teaching is seen as the "transmission of factual and procedural knowledge from one person to another."[4] Such knowledge is clearly known—*possessed* might be a better word—by the teacher in advance of the teaching situation. "It is," in Jackson's words, "knowledge 'presented' to a learner, rather than 'discovered' by him or her."[5] Since the knowledge passed on is clear and well-defined in advance, the teacher can evaluate the success of the teaching in a fairly accurate fashion "on the basis of comparison with the teacher's own knowledge or with some other model as found in a textbook or some other instructional materials."[6]

The transformative tradition, on the other hand, is aimed at bringing about "a transformation of one kind or another in the person being taught."[7] Transformative education is usually seen as "more deeply integrated and ingrained within the psychological makeup of the student"[8] than the accomplishments of mimetic education, and in general the

transformative tradition is more often associated with religious education than is the mimetic.[9]

Jewish educators want to encourage the transformative dimension
of teaching because the ultimate mission of most Jewish education is far
broader than helping students acquire mastery of a subject matter. The
educational enterprise is linked directly to hopes for personal growth or
change in students, no matter what their age. By learning more, the argument goes, the students should grow as Jews, and not only in their capacity of being Jews with knowledge, with a greater grasp of concepts,
ideas, or skills. Jewish education ultimately is judged by its success or
lack of success in its greater mission, to nurture Jews with a deep and
living connection to being Jewish.

And yet at the same time, Jewish education is intensely bound up
with issues of Jackson's "mimetic" ideal. To be a Jew entails obligations
of knowledge and attainment of competencies. Indeed, one of the particular difficulties of our own times is the widespread feeling among
Jews that they lack the basic skills and simple information that was in
the past expected of members of the Jewish community.[10]

And more than these contemporary associations, it is fair to say that
many of the statements in the Jewish tradition about the nature of
teaching resemble the mimetic view. Hence the famous description in
the Mishnaic tractate Avot of four kinds of students:

> There are four types of people who sit before the sages: [They
> can be compared to] a sponge, a funnel, a strainer, and a sieve.
> A sponge soaks up everything; a funnel lets in at one end and
> lets out at the other; a strainer lets out the wine and retains the
> lees; a sieve lets out the coarse meal and retains the choice
> flour.[11]

In praising Rabbi Eliezer ben Hyrcanus (he who "if put at one end
of a scale, and all the other sages at the other, the scale would weigh in
Eliezer's direction"!),[12] the same tractate describes him as "a plastered
cistern that loses not a drop."[13]

Similarly, we have the story of the death of the same Rabbi Eliezer.
Eliezer has essentially been banished by the rabbinic authorities over a
serious disagreement concerning his legal rulings. Finally, at the end of
his life, a group of the sages comes to visit him while he lies on his
deathbed. He turns to them and exclaims: "Woe for my two arms, that
are like two scrolls of the Torah and that are about to depart from the

world. For were all the seas ink, and all the reeds quills, and all the people, scribes, they would not suffice to write all the Scripture and Mishnah I learned . . . and my pupils have taken no more than a paintbrush takes from the tube."[14] For Eliezer, Torah is a kind of sacred possession, something one is able to pass on or not, given the particular circumstances.

Finally, the Talmud describes the case of the conflict between Rabbah and R. Joseph over which would be chosen as head of the Academy. The decision went to R. Joseph, since he was viewed as a "Sinai," one who knows the traditions of the past, as opposed to Rabbah, who was viewed as an *oker harim* (literally, "an uprooter of mountains")—known for his keen mind and ability to forge *new* decisions.[15]

In all these examples, the mimetic tradition powerfully informs the thinking of the texts about the nature of education. We "have" Torah, and we pass it on. All these seem to be talking about learning as acquisition of a particular "it" that is handed over to the student. Although it appears to me that the mimetic tradition does dominate this literature, there are other views found within the Jewish tradition as well—texts in which the tradition is seen as creative, dynamic, and multifaceted.[16] As I mentioned earlier, Jewish educators are caught between two opposing views, well documented in traditional texts as well as in contemporary educational thinking.

For Jewish education, this is made even more complicated by the fact that "mimetic" has another meaning as well. Beyond Jackson's notion of "transmission of factual and procedural knowledge from one person to another," in Judaism (and I imagine in most other religious traditions as well) mimesis is the act of imitating the behavior of one's teachers. We learn to be good Jews by watching what other good Jews do—the way they study and learn, certainly, but also the way that they conduct even the smallest details of their lives. This idea is certainly present in later movements within Judaism, such as Hasidism and Mussar, but has its clear roots back in the rabbinic period.[17]

Here, in essence, the mimetic and the transformative merge. We imitate, we do precisely what the master does, in order to transform our inner self, to become what the master has already become. We transform the inner by the outer gesture—we watch the way the master ties his shoes, we follow him to the bathhouse, we even hide beneath his bed. And we learn to extrapolate from shoes to other domains that the rabbi has not even taught us.

Of course, the issue is made even more complicated by the fact that for Judaism, a fundamental religious act *is* learning. Every day, Jews recite a rabbinic passage in the traditional prayer book, asserting that the study of Torah is equal to a whole variety of other commandments, including the honoring of parents, visiting the sick, and devotion in prayer. Studying Torah in its various guises is not simply a matter of learning the *whats* and *hows* of being Jewish. Studying is the essence of being a Jew. It defines who one is. Hence, Jewish learning is not only the instrumental gaining of skills, knowledge, and competencies. It is the religious act par excellence. Religious education is not only a preparation for what will come later; it is *being a Jew,* realizing one's Jewishness, in the very act of studying. Especially in a religious culture as literary as the Jewish tradition is, study goes to the heart of membership in the religious world of being a Jew.

•   •   •

As a Jewish teacher, then, I am caught between two different and powerful goals. Like Bailyn, I live in the mimetic mode: I wish to make sure that students know what is to be known—whether that be how to light the Hanukkah candles, how the medieval commentators understood a verse from the Bible, or what the conflicts between Herzl and the other early Zionists were. At the same time, if mimetic mastery of information were the end result of my teaching—and nothing else—wouldn't I have failed? Isn't the Jewish teacher's task to help students engage in their own personal encounter with text, deed, tradition, and history?

Our perception of the ultimate goals of Jewish education matters a great deal when we try to imagine ourselves as "good teachers" or when we try to envision or create programs and settings in which "good teachers" are prepared. Consider, for example, the following comment about teaching by a contemporary literary theorist, Robert Scholes:

> Our job is not to produce "readings" for our students but to give them the tools for producing their own. For me the ultimate hell at the end of all our good New Critical intentions is textualized in the image of a brilliant instructor explicating a poem before a class of stupefied students. . . . Our job is *not* to intimidate students with our own superior textual production; it is to show them the codes upon which all textual production depends, and to encourage their own textual practice.[18]

Scholes is talking quite passionately about a mode of teaching once common to university literature departments, and perhaps still done today. The teacher, particularly the talented textual interpreter, stands before the class in all the splendor of his (and, at least for the time that Scholes is talking about, it almost always was "his") "New Critical" armament: displaying his ability to dazzle the class with close readings of the literary work, particularly the complex web of meanings embodied in the structure and form of the text. New Criticism was particularly susceptible to the type of teaching described by Scholes because it viewed the act of criticism—the act of reading—as essentially concerned with the uncovering of textual meaning, and meaning was to be found in that which lay beneath the surface of the text. As one scholar has described it:

> [M]eaning was clearly not a matter merely of reading and understanding the paraphrasable content of a literary text. The fact that meaning could not be discussed independently of the form of a work made it virtually beyond paraphrase. . . . .
>
> Since the meaning of a literary text could not be expressed directly, what the New Critic sought to demonstrate was how the formal and semantic elements of a work interacted to manifest the underlying structure of the work's meaning.[19]

Such an approach to reading leads naturally to modes of teaching in which the instructor becomes the dazzling performer: as Scholes put it, the "brilliant instructor explicating a poem before a class of stupefied students" who cannot see the hidden structural complexities of the literary work before them. Because the work's meanings are always beneath the surface, only the teacher can see with full clarity what needs to be seen. Thus, the job of the teacher easily becomes presenting what he knows, rather than eliciting from students their own constructions of the texts' meanings. And, as Scholes adds, the passing of New Criticism out of academic mode has not lessened the temptations to teach in the ways that he has described: "And when I see this very icon [of the teacher] being restored to the same position within the same ivied halls, by certain disciples of Derrida—I could weep with frustration."[20] Contemporary literary theorists, with their even more arcane readings, occasionally anti-readings, of literary works, are perhaps even more guilty of the sin he has described.

But what precisely is that pedagogic sin? Obviously, to begin with, Scholes has exaggerated his case to make a point. Many teachers who viewed themselves as New Critics or were influenced by New Critical modes of reading, saw their task not as performance, but as encouraging responses from students about the texts that were being discussed. In my life, I have had many teachers who clearly saw themselves as encouraging close reading in us the students, rather than showing off their greater competency before us.

But even setting that aside, even accepting for a moment Scholes's portrait of the New Critical teacher from hell, what are we to make of it? When I read Scholes's description of the university teacher, what does it bring to mind? On the one hand, I am filled with sympathy for his point of view; but on the other, I hesitate, for I remember great teachers whom I have had who looked a lot like Scholes's description. And yet I would still call them great. Perhaps lurking slightly under the surface of Scholes's description is a different kind of sin that he sees in his example—pride or arrogance or immodesty. These are qualities that are unpleasant to find in any teacher, and if that's what he means, I may agree with him. (Though it certainly raises an interesting question: Is it possible to be both a good teacher and an arrogant one?) But there is something else going on here: Can't we say that there is something powerful and positive in the educational experience of sitting at the feet of a truly learned or inventive mind? Can't part of learning be the veneration of wisdom or brilliance? Perhaps Scholes ignores this possibility because he is writing about secular contexts. But for those working in a religious tradition—certainly, a tradition like Judaism—the experience of studying with a person who has attained a great deal of learning must be part of our definition of at least one kind of great teacher.

For example, we may believe—and find in the educational literature—that adult learners prefer "collaborative" models of education, settings in which they learn from one another, rather than from the teacher.[21] Yet in religious settings, it is not uncommon to find that learners want to learn in a teacher-centered environment, perhaps precisely because such situations seem to suggest a kind of religious truth. Such teachers emanate an aura of authority, which is what the adult learner may be seeking when turning to a religious class rather than to a Great Books discussion group or a course in pottery making.

The differences between the situations of general education, such as discussed by Scholes, and those of religious, particularly Jewish, education, are only partially indicated by the example of one's conception of the nature of a teacher and a teacher's role. The question of the ultimate aims of teaching—as I have noted earlier—may differ significantly for Jewish or general education as well. But the modes of pedagogy that we see in classrooms, in either context, are in important ways expressive of the teacher's larger vision of education—its purposes (whether in the mode of Bailyn, Oakeshott, or others) and its means.[22]

There is a great deal that we can learn by exploring the way in which some of these issues have been treated in contemporary general education, seeing the implications for our work in Jewish education, and also paying careful attention to the differences as well. In that spirit, I want to turn to a body of literature that seems to me quite relevant to the work of Jewish education: the research on secondary-school English teachers conducted by Pamela L. Grossman. Grossman's work—originally done as a doctoral dissertation at Stanford University—has appeared in a number of interesting articles and in a book, *The Making of a Teacher*, which appeared in 1990.[23]

Grossman studied six beginning secondary-school English teachers, paying particular attention to the relationship between knowledge of subject matter and the act of teaching that subject matter. As part of the large "Knowledge Growth in a Profession" project led by Lee Shulman, Grossman was interested in the "pedagogical content knowledge"[24] of the teachers she was studying, namely—in Shulman's words—"that special amalgam of content and pedagogy that is uniquely the province of teachers, their own special form of professional understanding."[25] Grossman herself described her project as an exploration of "the nature of pedagogical content knowledge in English among beginning teachers and the role of subject-specific teacher education coursework in contributing to graduates' knowledge and beliefs about teaching English."[26] What do beginning teachers know and believe about the subject they teach, and how do knowledge and beliefs influence their actual teaching practice?

For those of us interested in the teaching of Jewish texts, it is obvious that a serious study of the teaching of literature should have implications for the way that we think about our work. I now want to turn to the contributions that Grossman's work might offer us and then explore some of the limitations of translating such work for Jewish education. These limitations are in themselves illuminating about the nature of Jewish text learning.

Grossman has looked carefully at the importance of a teacher's knowledge of subject matter in the act of teaching. This approach to knowledge, focusing as it does on pedagogical content knowledge, goes a long way beyond the approach to subject-matter knowledge that characterized earlier research on teachers and teaching. That earlier research "found little or no relationship between teachers' subject-matter knowledge and either pupil achievement or general teaching performance."[27] But, as Grossman points out, those findings may "tell us as much about our difficulties in conceptualizing the role of subject-matter knowledge in teaching as about the relationship between knowledge and teaching itself."[28] What is far more significant for teaching than how many courses in the subject one took in college or how much information one knows when judged by a standardized test is what Grossman calls the teacher's "orientation" to the subject matter being taught.

Grossman uses "orientation" as an inclusive term that encompasses Joseph Schwab's notion of the "substantive" and "syntactic" structures of a discipline. But orientation, as we shall see, adds another element as well. As described by Schwab, the substantive structures of a discipline are the large organizing interpretive frames that are used for "defining, bounding, and analyzing the subject matters they investigate."[29] They are the lenses through which the entire field is understood. In literature, these might include substantive structures such as New Criticism, feminist criticism, or structuralism. In Bible, they might encompass those scholars who view the Bible through the lens of the ancient Near East, such as E. A. Speiser or Jacob Milgrom, or those who primarily use a literary approach to the text, such as Robert Alter or the contemporary Israeli Bible scholar Yair Zakovitch.[30]

The syntactic structures are the "different methods of verification and justification of conclusions"[31]—in other words, those tools that scholars use to introduce new knowledge to a field and the canons by which evidence is viewed as acceptable or not. These might include the use of replicable laboratory experiments in science, historical documents in literature and history, or logical proofs in mathematics and philosophy. Different substantive structures may call for different syntactic tools—thus, archaeological evidence may be of greater importance to a Bible scholar such as Speiser than to one such as Alter, though most academic fields will share certain assumptions about what constitutes legitimate or illegitimate ways to generate new knowledge.

Grossman, however, adds an important dimension to Schwab's emphasis on knowledge by recognizing the importance of teachers' beliefs about the subject matter as well, "since it is frequently the case that teachers treat their beliefs as knowledge."[32] Unlike knowledge, "beliefs rely heavily on affective and personal evaluations" of teachers, and "[i]f knowledge depends on meeting criteria such as the canons of evidence [that are] part of a teacher's syntactic knowledge, [a] teacher's beliefs are often justified or held for reasons that do not meet those criteria or follow those canons."[33]

"Orientation," as a term, then, encompasses aspects of both the knowledge and belief sides of a teacher's relationship to the subject matter. An orientation represents the "English teachers' interpretive stance . . . toward literature [and] becomes important in understanding their goals for instruction, curricular choices, instructional assignments, and classroom questions."[34] "More than a casual attitude towards the subject matter, an orientation towards literature represents a basic organizing framework for knowledge about literature."[35]

In her work, Grossman delineates three main orientations to a literary text: a text-based approach, a context-based approach, and a reader response-based approach. These three basic perspectives correspond roughly, in her view, to "three of the most common orientations towards literature"[36] in contemporary literary theory. It is important to point out that here Grossman oversimplifies a complex situation in present-day intellectual life quite a bit. "Context-based" literary criticism, for example, becomes a catchall for "theoretical models from outside English, such as Marxist or psychoanalytical theories,"[37] as well as approaches that emphasize the biography and intention of the writer and the cultural milieu in which the work appeared.

Similarly, the "reader-response" criticism of Grossman's triad encompasses in a single term all the various modes of textual reading that might go under that rubric. As Jane P. Tompkins put it in her introduction to one of the oft-cited anthologies of this literary approach, "reader-response criticism is not a conceptually unified critical position."[38] Indeed, "a variety of theoretical orientations" can be termed reader-response criticism: "New Criticism, structuralism, phenomenonology, psychoanalysis, and deconstructionism shape their definitions of the reader, of interpretation, and of the text."[39]

If, as Grossman claims—and here I wholeheartedly agree—"how high school teachers learn to read literature influences how they themselves will teach literature to their own students,"[40] then certainly we need to keep in mind all the various possible approaches that these future teachers may have encountered in their own undergraduate training. A student who has come under the influence of Derrida's approach to the text will certainly differ from one who has been taught by devotees of Wolfgang Iser or Stanley Fish. To place all these approaches and others, too, under the loose banner of "reader-response" seems to smooth over differences far more radically than is warranted.

Yet ultimately, I believe that there are two considerations in Grossman's argument that outweigh the objections that I have raised above. First, my reservations about Grossman's categories are essentially brought from the world of theory, and Grossman makes no claims—or no sustained claims, at any rate—about making a theoretical case. She is instead generalizing based on empirical data. She has a group of teachers in her study who, when interviewed and observed, appear to fit into the rough categories of text-centered, context-centered, and reader-response-centered orientations. Moreover, the teachers themselves were not interested in the niceties of these theoretical distinctions; those are the "battles" that take place "in the upper echelons of higher education."[41]

But beyond the empirical argument—the position that the teachers in the study are simply not involved in the debates of contemporary literary theory—one might even argue on theoretical grounds that Grossman's use of these terms is justified. That is, the three broad categories that she brings are useful rubrics for characterizing the substantive and syntactical structures of the field called English literature, despite their oversimplifications. They are a "practical" approach to the theoretical dilemma, in Schwab's sense of the practical as "always something taken as concrete and particular and treated as indefinitely susceptible to circumstance."[42]

Even a work that tries to tease out the various complicated distinctions among contemporary approaches to literature will find it "practical" to employ overarching simplifications as well. Thus Terry Eagleton, in his well-known book *Literary Theory: An Introduction*, writes, "One might very roughly periodize the history of modern literary theory in three stages: a preoccupation with the author (Romanticism and nineteenth century); an exclusive concern with the text (New Criticism); and a marked shift of attention to the reader over recent years."[43] Indeed, his three periods resemble to a large extent Grossman's categories.

The concept of orientation itself has a good deal to say about the situation of Jewish education, particularly in regard to the issues raised at the beginning of this paper. An orientation is a description not of a teacher's "method" in some technical meaning of the word, but in a deeper sense, of a teacher's most powerful conceptions and beliefs about the field he or she is teaching. It is the living expression of the philosophical questions with which we began: What is my view of the aims of education, and how as a teacher do I attain those aims?

To say, as did one of the teachers studied by Grossman, that "the most important thing for me in literature is not any psychoanalysis, it's not any of that . . . it's *explication de texte*"[44] is to express a specific notion of what teaching literature is about. It is a conception that allows one to judge one's successes or failures as a teacher and to judge students as well. As Grossman puts it, "from Jake's [the teacher quoted above] perspective, studying English involves studying a text in great depth, exploring the language and its multiple meanings"; another teacher in her study views English "as a vehicle both for teaching necessary skills and for fostering self-awareness."[45] Yet another's "preference is less for the critical and analytical aspects of English and more for what she terms the human aspect of literature."[46] Each of the positions articulated presents a different conception of goals and aspirations. Each will lead toward different specific teaching activities in the classroom.

Yet it is hard to know exactly what lies behind these orientations, what holds them together, what roots them. Because Grossman's work is built upon an empirical study, she is obliged only to describe the reality that she encountered and not to comment on what goals and practices might be desirable and why. How, after all, do these teachers come to have these orientations? The origin of an individual's orientation is not entirely clear. Grossman attributes it to "a probable combination of personal values and disciplinary training."[47] It seems to me that an orientation may also reflect personality traits, temperament, and a person's self-understanding of what one is good at doing.

From reading her descriptions, it seems that most teachers come to their orientations almost accidentally, with little reflection and even less philosophical inquiry. Israel Scheffler has argued, in contrast, that philosophy has an important role to play in the preparation of teachers. Although Scheffler does not use the term "orientation" (his article was written years before Grossman's research), he articulates the view that teachers need to be able to anchor their teaching in something more than habit or personal preference:

[The educator] cannot define his role simply as it is given by received traditions: he must be prepared to justify his perpetuation or alteration of them as a consequence of his efforts. This means that the process of clarifying his objectives has a critical and normative aspect to it. He needs, of course, to strive for a clear grasp of the form of thought embodied in the tradition to which he is heir. But in taking on the responsibility of educational transmission, he assumes the obligation of evaluating whatever it is in that tradition he elects to perpetuate. At the risk of oversimplification, we may say that he requires not only a descriptive but a critical clarification of the forms of thought represented by his subject.[48]

The fact that most teachers do not root their orientations in philosophical inquiry about the subject matter comes as little surprise to anyone who has spent time working in Jewish education, where the situation may be more problematic than that described by Grossman. After all, Grossman's young teachers have rather well-defined conceptions of the purposes of teaching, even if they be far less philosophically developed than what Scheffler might desire. For teachers in Jewish education, many of whom have even less academic background in their subject area than the teachers whom Grossman studied, confusion about goals is likely to be far more profound.[49]

•   •   •

But setting the question of origins asides, it is fair to ask why this is important at all, and how does an understanding of teachers' orientations help improve education? I would suggest three possible answers.

First, the issue of orientations, as I have mentioned above, is directly related to the actualities of pedagogic practice. Grossman shows the way that an individual teacher's orientation will deeply influence much of what takes place in his or her planning and execution of lessons:

> For example, one of the novice English teachers, Colleen, believed that the text was central to critical literary analysis; interpretations had to be rooted in evidence from the text. Another teacher, Martha, believed that the reader's subjective response to a work was the locus for interpretation. Representing, to some extent, different conceptions of interpretation in literature, and mirroring competing substantive structures, the differences in these two teachers' orientations corresponded to differences in the literature they chose to teach, as well as in their goals for instruction and choices of activities and assignments.[50]

If we wish to influence actual classroom practice, there is little doubt that we need to address the issue of orientation. "Orientation" represents an amalgam of a teacher's knowledge and beliefs about the subject matter. Hence, if we look at the "knowledge" elements of orientation, particularly the issues of substantive and syntactic structure, I believe that it is fair to argue that teachers who have not explored the structures of their discipline are at a great disadvantage in thinking about how to teach that discipline to others. As Schwab puts it, "To know what structures underlie a given body of knowledge is to know what problems we shall face in imparting this knowledge."[51] And, on the other side, if we look at teachers' "beliefs" about subject matter, a teacher who has not confronted his or her underlying assumptions, prejudices, emotions, and aims about a subject matter will teach in a much less effective and well-defined way. Self-reflection on one's beliefs and where these beliefs come from is a key element in improving one's practice as a teacher, both for those in preservice preparation programs and in professional development programs when they are out in the field.[52] An orientation is a real-life actualization of a teacher's underlying goals.

Orientations may play a second role as well. For those teachers who come into the field lacking a strong background of knowledge or training (as many do in Jewish education), a knowledge of orientations—for example, to the teaching of Bible—may give the teacher breadth in the absence of "depth" of subject-matter knowledge. Orientations might allow teachers to have a bird's-eye view that would help them to organize the subject matter for the student.

Third, I would add that an understanding of orientations also has important implications for schools—for example, in the way that a school might view its faculty makeup. For some schools, a variety of orientations would be a value; for others, having a coherence of orientations may be more desirable. For Jewish education, the implications of such considerations are clear: a community day school might want a wide range of orientations to text represented among the faculty; a denominational school may want to limit its faculty to certain types of orientations. A clearer understanding of teachers' orientations will help schools evaluate the relationship of the teaching going on in the school to the school's larger goals and vision.[53] Finally, it is clear that a deeper engagement with issues of orientation has important implications for teacher preparation programs: "As we begin to understand more about the role prior subject-matter knowledge plays in teaching, teacher educators . . . must grapple with how prospective teachers can best acquire the knowledge of their subjects they will need for teaching."[54]

Grossman has shown that while the teachers in her study tended to have a "dominant orientation," they also "may include elements of other orientations as well."[55] One way that teacher education programs can help improve the quality of teaching is to aim at developing within their students what has been called "flexible subject-matter understanding":

> Beginning teachers must develop a flexible, thoughtful, and con-
> ceptual understanding of their subject matter if they are to cre-
> ate or choose representations that enable pupils with diverse
> knowledge, experience, expectations, and values to develop sim-
> ilar understandings. "Flexible" implies that teachers need to
> know how a given phenomenon or event is related to other phe-
> nomena or events both within and outside their field. . . .
> "Thoughtful" means that teachers must understand how
> knowledge in the field is generated and verified and be aware of
> competing ideas that have been advanced to explained observed
> relationships. "Conceptual" implies that the teacher compre-
> hends the fundamental ideas and relationships that underlie in-
> terpretations of particular phenomena or events.[56]

In her empirical study of students in two teacher preparation pro-
grams for Jewish education, Gail Dorph examined the issue of flexible subject-matter knowledge for prospective Bible teachers. She argued for the

> importance of alternative structures of the disciplines . . . [a]
> framework that will allow teacher educators to help teachers
> learn *how to learn* and not just *what to teach*. It does not as-
> sume that teachers will become biblical scholars and be able to
> add new knowledge to the field of biblical studies, but rather
> that they will come to recognize alternative ways of looking at
> the text and understanding its meanings. It assumes that teach-
> ers will be eclectic in terms of their use of scholarly information.
> Using these approaches as interpretive lenses for viewing the
> text, syntactic knowledge will become a pedagogic tool.[57]

There is a direct relationship between a teacher's orientation and the openness of such a teacher to different kinds of "scholarly information," to use Dorph's phrase. This case is argued from a different point of view in Beverly Gribetz's study of the relationship between scholarly approaches to Talmud and the uses that a teacher may make of such approaches in teaching Talmud to children. Gribetz takes three specific talmudic texts and shows that in each case, certain pedagogic difficulties could be overcome if the teacher preparing these texts were familiar with different scholarly approaches to talmudic research. Each text called for a different approach, and a teacher who did not have the range of knowledge—who was limited by the specific approach of his or her orientation—would face problems in teaching the text. As Gribetz puts it, "a strong familiarity with the diverse types of advanced Talmudic scholarship is valuable, if not essential, for the competent teacher of Talmud."[58]

Gribetz adds a new dimension to our discussion: in addition to the importance of "flexibility," as argued by Dorph and by McDiarmid, Ball, and Anderson, Gribetz shows that the texts being learned may themselves "call out" for diverse scholarly approaches. It is crucial, she argues, "for the teacher of beginners to become acquainted with a variety of scholarly methodologies in order to be able to find and choose one that will best come to grips with or translate into one's curricular, pedagogic or didactic concerns."[59]

Thus, to use Grossman's example of English literature, it may be that the "right" orientation for teaching a particular Shakespeare sonnet should be determined not because of a teacher's personal preference but because the text itself demands the use of a "reader-response," "text-based," or "context-oriented" approach. Certainly, many texts are susceptible to a variety of different orientations and could be taught effectively using one of a large number of them. But teachers who possess a range of possibilities, a spectrum of orientations at their command, have many more pedagogic possibilities before them.

·   ·   ·

As we have shown, the idea of orientations in Grossman's work has significant implications for Jewish education and the preparation of Jewish teachers. We have seen that it is directly connected to the issue of the goals of Jewish education and the implementation of those goals in teaching practice, but before we conclude let us reflect on some of the challenges presented by trying to apply categories from the world of general education to the teaching of Jewish sources. Or, to put it another way, in what way does teaching English literature differ from teaching Bible, Talmud, and other texts of the Jewish tradition? Let me suggest three specific problems.

First, we need to encounter what might be called the problem of genre. Grossman's orientations are, as I have stated above, essentially stripped-down versions of a number of different aspects of contemporary literary theory. But the focus on text, context, and reader cuts across the many subgenres of English literature—lyric poetry, epic poetry, drama, novel, and so on. These same three terms may be applicable to classical Jewish writings as well, but because the genres of Jewish texts are in general so different from those of Western literature, we have to wonder how much overlap actually exists. Where exactly does the Bible fit, in terms of genre? In fact, it appears to encompass a number of different literary forms: some, like biblical narrative, seem very close to mainstream Western literature; others, like biblical poetry, may or may not be close to what we usually mean by poetry;[60] and others, like prophetic writings and Proverbs, seem very different from mainstream literature.[61] (And if the Bible—a key cornerstone of much of Western literature—doesn't fit nicely within the genres of Western literature, what are we to say about the Talmud, the midrashic writings, or the Zohar!) Translating from an educational literature about Western literature to the writings of the Jewish tradition is not so simple.

A second way to see these complexities is to consider the word "belief" as it is used in general education and as it is applicable to Jewish education. In general education, the word "belief" encompasses a variety of possibilities, including what teachers may believe about the nature and aims of teaching, the purpose and function of schools, and the specific qualities of the discipline that they are teaching. All these elements are, of course, present in Jewish education as well.

But the word "belief" itself adds an additional dimension when we look at religious education. Although it is true, as Dorph points out, that contemporary educational research has shown the influence of beliefs about the nature of subject matter on prospective math teachers and novice history teachers,[62] it seems to me that the analogy to general education tells only part of the story. In Jewish education, the beliefs that teachers may hold about their subject matters are often tied inextricably to the largest beliefs of their personal lives, their religious faith, and behavior. One looks at the literature from general education and sees, as Dorph puts it, that

[t]hese same kinds of issues dealing with beliefs about the substantive and syntactic structures of the discipline also apply to Torah. . . . But beliefs about Torah have some unique characteristics that go beyond these substantive and syntactic stances. Underlying all of them is the issue of the nature of the document itself. Is [Torah] divine or human in origin? This is not an issue of syntactic approach.[63]

Finally, there is the matter of what I would call the problem of intention, namely, what is the purpose of studying these texts at all? Although there is, of course, a great deal of debate within the tradition about the purposes of Torah study, it is clear that Jewish texts are not to be studied simply for personal edification or entertainment, although they may also be that. The study of Jewish texts at its heart is viewed within the context of a religious obligation that often is aimed at leading the student toward certain kinds of behaviors (i.e., mitzvot) or, at the very least, at an involvement in a way of living within which study itself is a central element.[64] Although one can certainly find justifications for the study of the humanities within contemporary literature—for example, in the philosopher Martha Nussbaum's recent work[65]—the deep connection between text and life that is integral to Jewish religious education, no matter what the context, is not parallel to the situation of general education.

None of this is meant to deny the enormous amount that can be learned from the research that Grossman and others have done in general education. To begin with, this work points us in the direction of the need for more empirical studies about the way that teachers view teaching and the way that students do or do not learn what they are being taught. But aside from empirical studies, it is also clear that more work on a theory of practice also needs to be done: What are the models, the "orientations," that make sense in the various disciplines of Jewish education? How do they resemble and differ from those found in general education?

Orientations, viewed in one way, only relate to the *teacher's* perception of the discipline. Equally important is the way that the subject is perceived by the learner: What are the misunderstandings, preconceptions, and misconceptions that students bring with them to the study of any Jewish subject matter? What are the difficulties that they are likely to encounter in any particular discipline or even any particular text?

And, once we have ascertained all this, what, in Lee Shulman's words, are "the most useful forms of representation . . . the most powerful examples, explanations, and demonstrations—in a word, the ways of representing and formulating the subject that makes it comprehensible to others"?[66] What, for example, is best way to explain the nature of a "prooftext" to students first studying midrash? How do we deal with the apparent conflict between science and religion in teaching the first chapters of Genesis? What is the clearest explanation of the *Sefirot* to students first studying kabbalah? How do we explain the wicked son's question in teaching the Passover Haggadah? Later in this book, I will return to the issue of "representations" to explore ways that we might think about them in relationship to teaching the Bible.

Our explanations and demonstrations, the exercises we prepare for students, the cases we have them ponder, the examinations we give, the supplementary readings we assign, the projects we design—all will be deeply influenced by the specific orientations we bring to each of the Jewish disciplines. But until we begin to map out the theory of teaching practice and design classroom activities for different ages of students and the settings in which they are taught (what I have lately come to call the "Bible teaching genome project"), we will not have begun to address the way that our goals for Jewish education and the teaching practices we wish to encourage interact and meet. In the next chapter, I want to turn specifically to the question of orientations for the teaching of Bible. I want to examine some of the categories that Grossman has laid out for teaching literature and to see ways that they may be relevant to teaching the Bible. Moving beyond that, I want to suggest a kind of "pedagogical map" of orientations for teaching the Bible, using Grossman's tools but expanding them in directions located in the particularities of teaching the Bible.

Notes

1. Bernard Bailyn, quoted in Lawrence A. Cremin, *Public Education* (New York: Basic Books, 1976), p. 28.
2. The passage is from Michael Oakeshott's *Rationalism in Politics and Other Essays* (London: Methuen, 1962), as quoted in Paul Hirst's famous article "Liberal Education and the Nature of Knowledge," in Hirst's collection of papers, *Knowledge and the Curriculum* (London and Boston: Routledge & Kegan Paul, 1974), p. 52.

3. Philip W. Jackson, "The Mimetic and the Transformative: Alternative Outlooks on Teaching," in his *The Practice of Teaching* (New York: Teachers College Press, 1986), p. 116.
4. Ibid., p. 117.
5. Ibid.
6. Ibid., p. 118.
7. Ibid., p. 120.
8. Ibid., p. 121.
9. Ibid.
10. As long ago as 1969, Walter Ackerman raised this problem in his essay "Jewish Education—for What?" in the *American Jewish Yearbook* 70, pp. 3–36.
11. Mishnah, Avot 5:19.
12. Ibid., 2:12.
13. Ibid., 2:8.
14. *Avot d'Rabbi Natan* 25.
15. Babylonian Talmud, Berakhot 64a.
16. See my discussion in Holtz, *Finding Our Way: Jewish Texts and the Lives We Lead Today* (New York: Schocken, 1990), pp. 15–38.
17. See Arthur Green, "Typologies of Leadership and the Hasidic Zaddiq," in *Jewish Spirituality*, ed. Arthur Green (New York: Paulist, 1989), 2:127–56; and Immanuel Etkes, *Rabbi Israel Salanter and the Mussar Movement* (Philadelphia: Jewish Publication Society, 1993). For the rabbinic period, see Moses Aberbach, "The Relations between Master and Disciple in the Talmudic Age," in *Essays Presented to Chief Rabbi Israel Brodie*, ed. H. J. Zimmels (London: Soncino, 1977), 2:1–27.
18. Robert Scholes, *Textual Power* (New Haven: Yale University Press, 1985), pp. 24–25.
19. K. M. Newton, *Interpreting the Text* (New York and London: Harvester Wheatsheaf, 1990), p. 16.
20. Scholes, *Textual Power*, p. 24.
21. See, for example, S. B. Merriam, ed., *An Update on Adult Learning Theory* (San Francisco: Jossey-Bass, 1993); and M. H. Rossman and M. E. Rossman, *Applying Adult Development Strategies* (San Francisco: Jossey-Bass, 1990). For a study of contemporary Jewish adult education, see Paul Flexner, "Facilitating Adult Jewish Learning" (Ph.D. diss., Teachers College, Columbia University, 1995).
22. For a discussion of the implications for Jewish education of the idea that the means of education are not neutral, see Seymour Fox, "Toward a General Theory of Jewish Education," in *The Future of the American Jewish Community*, ed. David Sidorsky (New York: Basic Books, 1973), pp. 260–71.
23. Among others, see: Pamela L. Grossman, *The Making of a Teacher: Teacher Knowledge and Teacher Education* (New York: Teachers College Press, 1990);

idem, "What Are We Talking About Anyhow? Subject-Matter Knowledge of English Teachers," in *Advances in Research on Teaching*, ed. J. Brophy (JAI, 1991), 2:245–64; Pamela L. Grossman, Suzanne M. Wilson, and Lee S. Shulman, "Teachers of Substance: Subject-Matter Knowledge for Teaching," in *Knowledge Base for the Beginning Teacher*, ed. M. Reynolds (New York: Pergamon, 1989), pp. 23–36.

24. The term "pedagogical content knowledge" has become widely known in the field of education, thanks to Lee S. Shulman and his students and colleagues. See Shulman's oft-cited discussion in the influential article "Those Who Understand: Knowledge Growth in Teaching," *Educational Researcher* 15, no. 2 (1986): 4–14. Grossman points out that, to be sure, pedagogical content knowledge is not the only area of knowledge that is important for literature teachers to master, but it is the main focus of her inquiry.

25. Lee S. Shulman, "Knowledge and Teaching: Foundations of the New Reform," *Harvard Educational Review* 57, no. 1 (February 1987): 8.

26. Grossman, *The Making of a Teacher*, p. x.

27. Grossman, "What Are We Talking About Anyhow?" p. 258.

28. Ibid.

29. Joseph J. Schwab, "Education and the Structure of the Disciplines" (1961), in his collected essays, *Science, Curriculum, and Liberal Education*, ed. Ian Westbury and Neil J. Wilkof (Chicago: University of Chicago Press, 1978), p. 246.

30. Such as: E. A. Speiser, *Genesis*, Anchor Bible (Garden City, N.Y.: Doubleday, 1964); Jacob Milgrom, *Leviticus 1–16, A New Translation with Introduction and Commentary* (New York: Doubleday, 1991); Robert Alter, *The Art of Biblical Narrative* (New York: Basic Books, 1981); and Yair Zakovitch, *David: From Shepherd to Messiah* [in Hebrew] (Jerusalem: Yad Yitzhak Ben-Zvi, 1995).

31. Schwab, "Education and the Structure of the Disciplines," p. 246.

32. Grossman et al., "Teachers of Substance," p. 31.

33. Ibid.

34. Grossman, "What Are We Talking About Anyhow?" p. 247.

35. Ibid., p. 248.

36. Ibid., p. 247.

37. Ibid.

38. Jane P. Tompkins, ed., *Reader-Response Criticism: From Formalism to Post-Structuralism* (Baltimore: Johns Hopkins University Press, 1980), p. ix. See also Susan R. Suleiman and Inge Crosman, eds., *The Reader in the Text* (Princeton: Princeton University Press, 1980).

39. Tompkins, *Reader-Response Criticism*, p. ix.

40. Grossman, "What Are We Talking About Anyhow?" p. 247.

41. Ibid.

42. Joseph J. Schwab, "The Practical: A Language for Curriculum" (1970), in *Science, Curriculum, and Liberal Education*, ed. Westbury and Wilkof, p. 289.

43. Terry Eagleton, *Literary Theory: An Introduction*, 2d ed. (Oxford: Blackwell, 1996), p. 64.
44. Grossman, *The Making of a Teacher*, p. 20.
45. Ibid., p. 43.
46. Grossman, "What Are We Talking About Anyhow?" p. 251.
47. Ibid., p. 259.
48. Israel Scheffler, "Philosophy and the Curriculum," in his *Reason and Teaching* (London: Routledge & Kegan Paul, 1973), p. 38.
49. See the study by the Council for Initiatives in Jewish Education, *Policy Brief on the Background and Training of Teachers in Jewish Schools* (New York: Council for Initiatives in Jewish Education, 1994).
50. Grossman et al., "Teachers of Substance," p. 31.
51. Joseph J. Schwab, "Structure of the Disciplines: Meanings and Significances," in *The Structure of Knowledge and the Curriculum*, ed. G. W. Ford and Lawrence Pugno (Chicago: Rand McNally, 1964), p. 13.
52. On the issue of professional development of teachers and reflection on practice, see Barry W. Holtz, Gail Zaiman Dorph, and Ellen B. Goldring, "Educational Leaders as Teacher Educators," *Peabody Journal of Education* 72, no. 2 (fall 1997): 149–52.
53. See Seymour Fox, "From Theory to Practice in Jewish Education" (paper presented at the Twelfth World Congress of Jewish Studies, Jerusalem, 30 July 1997); Daniel Pekarsky, "The Place of Vision in Jewish Educational Reform," *Journal of Jewish Education* 63, nos. 1–2 (winter/spring 1997): 31–40.
54. Grossman, "What Are We Talking About Anyhow?" p. 260.
55. Ibid., p. 248.
56. G. Williamson McDiarmid, Deborah Loewenberg Ball, and Charles W. Anderson, "Why Staying One Chapter Ahead Doesn't Really Work: Subject-Specific Pedagogy," in *Knowledge Base for the Beginning Teacher*, ed. Reynolds, p. 198.
57. Gail Zaiman Dorph, "Conceptions and Preconceptions: A Study of Prospective Jewish Educators' Knowledge and Beliefs about Torah" (Ph.D. diss., Jewish Theological Seminary, 1993), pp. 226–27.
58. Beverly Gribetz, "On the Translation of Scholarship to Pedagogy: The Case of Talmud" (Ph.D. diss., Jewish Theological Seminary, 1995), p. 170.
59. Ibid., p. 28.
60. See the discussion in James L. Kugel, *The Idea of Biblical Poetry* (New Haven: Yale University Press, 1981), pp. 69–95.
61. See, for example, the discussion of whether there ever existed an Israelite national *epic* in Shemaryahu Talmon's "The Comparative Method in Biblical Interpretation," in his *Literary Studies in the Hebrew Bible* (Jerusalem: Magnes, 1993), pp. 44–48.
62. Dorph, "Conceptions and Preconceptions," p. 218.
63. Ibid., p. 68.

64. See the discussion of *Torah lishmah,* "study for its own sake," in Holtz, *Finding Our Way,* pp. 211–24; and in Michael Rosenak, *Roads to the Palace: Jewish Texts and Teaching* (Providence: Berghahn, 1995), pp. 231–34.

65. For example, Martha C. Nussbaum, *Cultivating Humanity* (Cambridge: Harvard University Press, 1997), and her *Poetic Justice* (Boston: Beacon, 1995).

66. Shulman, "Those Who Understand," p. 9.

CHAPTER THREE

Teaching the Bible:
Building a Conceptual Map

In the last chapter, I explored the ways that a teacher's stance in relation to the subject matter being taught might influence actual classroom practices. That stance represents a combination of knowledge and beliefs about the subject matter and expresses the teacher's "orientation" toward the subject, to use Pamela Grossman's term. I argued that, despite some reservations, the concept of teacher orientation clearly is a useful rubric for thinking about the teaching of Jewish texts. What I would like to do now is to turn away from focusing on the idea of orientation and to explore specific possible orientations toward the teaching of Bible that we might be able to identify. The goal is to see the ways that orientations might serve as a practical tool for Bible teachers. How might a "map" of Bible orientations help expand a teacher's perspective and improve the quality of teaching and learning in his or her classroom?

A good place to start, I would suggest, is with the three fundamental perspectives that Grossman identified as important in literary scholarship: the text-oriented, the context-oriented, and the reader-response-oriented approaches to reading—and teaching—texts. First we will see what these three points of view might mean for teaching texts outside the world of Jewish education—in general education—and then we will examine how what we learn from that exercise may be applied to teaching the Bible.

Three English Literature Lessons

To illustrate the point, I want to imagine a class outside the world of Jewish education—let us say, in the spirit of Grossman's work, a class of high school students studying English literature. Let us imagine three lessons that might be taught, each exemplifying a different orientation toward teaching texts.

Lesson One: Shakespeare, Sonnet 73

In the first lesson, the teacher hands out the following papers:

Shakespeare, "Sonnet 73"

That time of year thou mayst in me behold
When yellow leaves, or none, or few, do hang
Upon those boughs which shake against the cold,
Bare ruined choirs where late the sweet birds sang.
In me thou seest the twilight of such day
As after sunset fadeth in the west,
Which by and by black night doth take away,
Death's second self, that seals up all in rest.
In me thou seest the glowing of such fire
That on the ashes of his youth doth lie,
As the deathbed whereon it must expire,
Consumed with that which it was nourished by.
  This thou perceiv'st, which makes thy love more
    strong,
  To love that well which thou must leave ere long.

William Wordsworth, "Composed upon Westminster Bridge, September 3, 1802"

Earth has not anything to show more fair:
Dull would he be of soul who could pass by
A sight so touching in its majesty;
This City now doth, like a garment, wear
The beauty of the morning; silent, bare,
Ships, towers, domes, theaters, and temples lie
Open unto the fields, and to the sky;
All bright and glittering in the smokeless air.
Never did sun more beautifully steep
In his first splendor, valley, rock, or hill;
Ne'er saw I, never felt, a calm so deep!
The river glideth at his own sweet will:
Dear God! the very houses seem asleep;
And all that mighty heart is lying still!

1) The poem on the left above is written in the form known as an "English" or "Shakespearean" sonnet. Next to it you will find another poem, "Composed upon Westminster Bridge," written in the form known as an "Italian" or "Petrarchan" sonnet. Look at both poems and see if you can see the differences in form (not the content). Irrespective of the page layout, how many stanzas does each have? Where do they divide? What is the pattern of end words rhyming in each? Write your comments below:

2) *Place yourself in a group with two other people.* Each of you should share what you discovered about the formal structure of the poem and see if there is consensus. Note points of disagreement (or confusion) below:

3) *Remaining in your group.* Staying with Sonnet 73 (and setting "Composed upon Westminster Bridge" aside): Identify the dominant metaphor in each stanza. Consider the question of progressions or movement in the poem from stanza to stanza. Think about the representations of color, light, and quantity of time—do these change or move as the poem develops? Discuss in your group and write down some thoughts below:

The teacher in this lesson is conducting a "text-based" exploration of the poem. She is trying to vary her pedagogy by asking students to work both individually and in small groups. But more than that, she is working on some of the classic "New Critical" constructs of the relationship between form and meaning in literary works. Her intention in both the individual and small-group work is to get students first to notice the variations between the two sonnet forms (English and Italian) and then for the students to consider the ways that the forms might be appropriate to certain kinds of meanings. Perhaps, she is suggesting, certain forms work better with certain kinds of meaning. Perhaps poets choose the forms they use based on "semantic" rather than merely "formal" considerations.[1]

Thus, upon completing the worksheet exercises above, she begins a classroom discussion in which she asks the groups to analyze what they have learned from their investigations. She then guides them through a whole-class discussion in which the class looks at specific elements within the Shakespeare poem and how they function: how time is measured in increasingly smaller units (from season to part of a day to the last moments of a fire); how light grows dimmer as the sonnet moves forward; how the concern for human mortality grows as the poem progresses. She wants to deal with the ideas of death and rebirth, despair, and hope that are at the core of this sonnet. The original exercises done by the students lead naturally to this inclusive whole-class discussion.

As it progresses, the lesson has a number of different aims: first, students are to learn that literary works are to be studied with a certain ahistorical purity. They are to look at the text in its own terms. That is, virtually no "outside" information is given to them (aside from glossing some difficulties in Shakespeare's language and explaining the difference between the two sonnet forms). The text is meant to stand on its own and be read without a good deal of historical or contextual information. Second, students learn about the relationship between form and content; they learn, to use John Ciardi's oft-used phrase, "how a poem means."[2] The class analyzes the poem's meaning in the light of its language and form. Students learn skills of close reading and intellectual analysis, and the exercise of reading this poem is meant to stand as a model of how one reads virtually any poem.

Lesson Two: Shakespeare's *Merchant of Venice*

Now let us imagine a different lesson, also in the field of literature, done perhaps by a different teacher working with the same students. The subject is Shakespeare's *Merchant of Venice*. The teacher enters the room and refers the students to the following passage from the play:

Shylock:	Why look you, how you storm!
	I would be friends with you, and have your love,
	Forget the shames that you have stained me with,
	Supply your present wants, and take no doit
	Of usance for my moneys; and you'll not hear me,
	This is kind I offer.
Bassanio:	This were kindness.
Shylock:	This kindness will I show:
	Go with me to a notary; seal me there
	Your single bond, and, in a merry sport,
	If you repay me not on such a day,
	In such a place, such sum or sums as are
	Expressed in the condition, let the forfeit
	Be nominated for an equal pound
	Of your fair flesh, to be cut off and taken
	In what part of your body pleaseth me.
Antonio:	Content, in faith. I'll seal to such a bond,
	And say there is much kindness in the Jew.
Bassanio:	You shall not seal to such a bond for me!
	I'll rather dwell in my necessity

(1.3.134ff., Signet ed.)

The teacher continues: "Here Shylock seals a bond with Antonio (the merchant of Venice himself) concerning the repayment of a loan. From what part of the body is that pound of flesh to be taken?" From this passage, it appears that Shylock can take that flesh from wherever he wants it, a student points out. "True," the teacher responds, "but consider the following lines from later in the play":

Portia:	I pray you let me look upon the bond.
Shylock:	Here 'tis, most reverend Doctor, here it is.
Portia:	Shylock, there's thrice thy money off'red thee.
Shylock:	An oath, an oath! I have an oath in heaven.
	Shall I lay perjury upon my soul?
	No, not for Venice!
Portia:	Why, this bond is forfeit;
	And lawfully by this the Jew may claim
	A pound of flesh, to be by him cut off

> Nearest the merchant's heart. Be merciful,
> Take thrice thy money; bid me tear the bond.

Shylock: When it is paid, according to the tenour.
> It doth appear you are a worthy judge,
> You know the law, your exposition
> Hath been most sound: I charge you by the law,
> Whereof you are a well-deserving pillar,
> Proceed to judgement. By my soul I swear
> There is no power in the tongue of man
> To alter me. I stay here on my bond.

(4.1.224, Signet ed.)

The teacher continues: "Portia makes it clear that the pound of flesh will come from near Antonio's heart. Is that what Shylock really wants? Or is it Portia's interpretation of the arrangement that we are hearing?" The teacher then notes that in both cases, the text says "cut off"—an odd use of language, for wouldn't "cut out" be more appropriate to an area near the heart? "What," the teacher asks, "might 'cut out' suggest?" More like circumcision or castration, some students suggest. (Now, of course, we are not dealing with young children in this class!)

The class proceeds now with a presentation or mini-lecture conducted by the teacher. He points out that the word "flesh" in Shakespeare's time was a euphemism for the male sexual organ and that an Elizabethan audience attending a performance of the play would have heard and understood that implied pun. (*Romeo and Juliet* has a number of such puns on the word.) But we know the connections not just from the pun, but also from the sources behind the play. The teacher refers the students to excerpts from some of the earlier and contemporary works that appear to have influenced Shakespeare, such as the following passage from Alexander Silvayn's *The Orator* (1596), in which the Jew states:

> Neither am I to take that which he oweth me, but he is to deliver it to me. And especially because no man knoweth better than he where the same may be spared to the least hurt of his person, for I might take it in such a place as he might thereby happen to lose his life. What a matter were it then if I should cut of his privy members, supposing that the same would altogether weigh a just pound?[3]

As the presentation continues, the teacher points out that for a reader (or playgoer) in Shakespeare's time, an understanding of the play would be strongly influenced by certain shared values and social conventions—about Jews, Judaism, and the relationship between the "Old Testament" and the "New Testament" (as Christians express it). Shakespeare's readers (or better, his playgoing "viewers") would have believed that true circumcision is not, as Judaism has it, in the physical flesh, but in the heart, as Saint Paul's Epistle to the Romans expresses it. All this is the subtext of the play. This teacher's lesson suggests that the way to understand *The Merchant of Venice* is to understand it in its historical context, as Shakespeare himself might have intended it.

Here, quite obviously, we are looking at a very different kind of orientation to the teaching of Shakespeare. No longer the text "on its own," as we saw in Lesson One, but rather the text in its context. Our imaginary teacher has been much influenced by a recent book on Shakespeare, James Shapiro's *Shakespeare and the Jews,* and the understandings that the teacher brings to the class (and the historical texts, too) have been learned from Shapiro's work of scholarship.

Lesson Three: Two Twentieth-Century Poems

Finally, we have a third lesson. The teacher passes out the following:

Wallace Stevens, "The Snow Man"

One must have a mind of winter
To regard the frost and the boughs
Of the pine-trees crusted with snow;

And have been cold a long time
To behold the junipers shagged with ice,
The spruces rough in the distant glitter

Of the January sun; and not to think
Of any misery in the sound of the wind,
In the sound of a few leaves,

Which is the sound of the land
Full of the same wind
That is blowing in the same bare place

For the listener, who listens in the snow,
And, nothing himself, beholds
Nothing that is not there and the nothing that is.[4]

1) *Read the poem above to yourself.* On the back of this page or on a separate piece of paper, write your reflections on the following: Picture yourself "inside" this poem. Think about the metaphors and images used by Stevens. What happens to you, the reader, as you listen to the poem? What would you say is the dominant feeling(s) that the poem produces in you? What does the poem do to attain that effect? What ideas, emotions, images come to mind as you read the work?

2) Next you will find a poem, "The edge," by Richard Jones. *Read the poem to yourself.* Think about the following: What would you say that this poem is telling us about the way we lead or should lead our lives? If you were to take the poem seriously, if you were to listen to it as speaking directly to you, what would it mean about how you would lead your life?

Richard Jones, "The edge"

It doesn't have to be terrifying.
Sometimes it's simply curling your toes
over the end of the high dive,
bending your knees and lightly bouncing
up and down, as if your wings were fluttering.

Or it might be the moment when you're waiting—
Dawn—at the border—
For the man in the blue uniform
To hand back your passport,
to say it's all right to leap
from the train to the platform.

And after the flying and the splash,
after you haul your bag up on your shoulder,
it's safe to say that before long
you'll come to the edge of *something*
and have to leap again.

Maybe it's someone you didn't see
by the pool, wearing a flowered bathing suit—
maybe the love of your life.
Or maybe it's a museum with one painting
that finally explains everything.

And even if death *is* waiting,
you can still love
the perfect fit of the doorknob

in your hand as you open the door.
You can still search for the immortal
painting and buy your postcards of it
to send all over the world.
You can leap
and let the water hold you,
throwing one hand over the other,
hoisting yourself up
to dry your body in the sun
You can lift your rucksack—
the road rolling away before you—
and walk on joyfully,
going forward, forever leaping,
loving the high dive as well as the bottom stair,
loving the held breath, loving the tired feet.[5]

In this lesson, there is very little directed discussion by the teacher. When the class has finished writing, students share their answers in small groups. In some cases, students do not share their responses at all because the teacher has told the class that no one will be required to show what he or she has written to anyone else. The responses are private, though the students know that the teacher will read them later.

What we see in this teacher is a version of the reader-response orientation that Grossman has described. For this teacher, literature is essentially connected to personal response from the students. This teacher's experiences in college literature classes were shaped by professors who were influenced by postmodern approaches to reading. Moreover, the teacher remembers that her own best experiences in high school were those in which the teacher called on the students "to relate" to the poem at hand, and these moments resonated with her own personality and interests.

Three English Literature Lessons: What Have We Seen?

The lessons we have just seen represent possible expressions of Grossman's notion of three different orientations to the teaching of texts. We might lay them out in the following chart:

Teaching Texts: Chart One

What is the text?	Shakespeare, Sonnet 73 ("That Time of Year")	Shakespeare, *The Merchant of Venice*	Stevens, "The Snow Man" Jones, "The edge"
Orientation shorthand	Literary Criticism ("New Criticism")	Historical, contextual, biographical	Personal reader-response
What is the orientation?	The text stands on its own. We learn "how the poem means" (its formal structures). We analyze its meaning in the light of its language and form.	Understanding the play requires knowing how it would have been understood in Shakespeare's time. We use "external" tools = anthropology, historical methods. Analysis of texts.	Literature is related to personal meaning. We learn who we are from reading others. We explore the reader's experience qua reader. Reactions, reflections on methods by which text affects reader.
What is the "warrant" (for orientation)? E.g., specific scholarly resources behind it?	"New Criticism" E.g., T. S. Eliot, John Crowe Ransom, Cleanth Brooks, John Ciardi	Cultural studies; literary history E.g., James Shapiro	Reader-response criticism E.g., Stanley Fish
What is the point (of lesson)?	Learning sonnet structure; investigating: Are formal structures aesthetic or semantic? Exploring the "argument" of the poem.	Viewing "pound of flesh" issue in the light of Shakespeare's time. How do sources of the period teach us about the play? Conversely, how does the play teach us about the period?	Each of us knows the poem in our own way. We explore the way the poem affects us (as a way of discovering its meanings).
What are the strategies (of the lesson)?	Analyze structures individually and in groups via writing and conversation. Compare to other poem ("Composed upon Westminster Bridge"). Questions and discussion led by teacher.	Examine and analyze source materials with presentation by teacher. Use original documents where possible.	Writing reactions. Importance of self-reflection. Opportunity to share with others in groups or pairs.

The chart on the previous page tries to give a bird's-eye view of our three imaginary English literature lessons. I have tried here to map out how the lessons work, what they aim at accomplishing, and what the "warrant" is for each of these approaches, that is, in what way one can base the educational work on generally recognizable approaches to the subject of English literature, particularly as it is studied in the university. The structures of the lessons are clearly drawn here, but I would like to point out one subtle but important distinction that needs to be recognized.

If we look more closely at our third category, we see that the lesson "Two Twentieth-Century Poems" includes in actuality two different kinds of orientations. The lesson on the Stevens poem does indeed resemble the work of contemporary "reader-response" critics. In asking the questions that were asked—such as "What happens to you, the reader, as you listen to the poem? What would you say is the dominant feeling(s) that the poem produces in you?"—the teacher was following in the line of critics like Stanley Fish, for whom, in the words of one commentator, "reading is not a matter of discovering what the text means, but a process of experiencing what it does to you."[6] Reader-response criticism "would argue that a poem cannot be understood apart from its results. Its 'effects,' psychological and otherwise, are essential to any accurate description of its meaning, since that meaning has no effective existence outside of its realization in the mind of a reader."[7] The focus, in other words, in reader-response criticism is on the experience of reading the text.[8]

All that seems fine, but what about the questions concerning the Jones poem? For example, "What would you say that this poem is telling us about the way we lead or should lead our lives?" Is this still "reader-response criticism" in the way the term has come to be used? Haven't we gone beyond the "effects" of the poem on the reader to a completely different realm?

Here our questions resemble those of some of the teachers, described by Pamela Grossman, who saw the teaching of literature less as an exercise in textual analysis and more of an invitation for students to explore both their own experiences and ideas beyond the realm of their personal experience; these teachers' focus was not on the literary text but on the student in relation to that text.[9] These particular teachers (as opposed to the teachers who saw *explication de texte* as the core of their teaching) "believed that enabling

students to make connections between literature and their own experience was the major purpose for teaching literature at the high school
level."[10]

It seems clear that another orientation is at work here. We might
call it "personalization," since its primary focus is on the personal
relevance of the written text to the life of the individual reader. Personalization is related to some of the newer trends in contemporary
literary criticism that go by a variety of names—"personal criticism,"
"autobiographical criticism," and "the New Belletrism," to mention
just three.[11] "Personal criticism," in the words of one practitioner,
"entails an explicitly autobiographical performance within the act
of criticism."[12] The inclusion of one's autobiographical perspective into the critical mix seems to be the crucial element of this
approach to writing about texts; in some cases, the text is merely the
occasion for the personal rumination. But a critic's self-reflection on
his or her own life story (as seems most common in this writing) is
substantially different from the kind of "personalization" exhibited
in the lesson on the Richard Jones poem above. The point in that kind
of teaching is not to authorize autobiographical reflection, but to
draw the text and the student closer together. In a personalist orientation, the key question is the one posed by our third teacher above: "If
you were to take the poem seriously, if you were to listen to it as
speaking directly to you, what would it mean about how you would
lead your life?"

Personalization also has certain important connections to what
is sometimes called the "ethical criticism" of writers such as Wayne
C. Booth and Martha Nussbaum, but there are certain significant
differences as well. Later in this book, I shall try to explore these
distinctions, but for the time being, let us add "personalization" to
the chart as yet another "orientation," one that is evidenced (significantly, I believe) far more in real-life educational practice than it is in
literary studies.[13]

Keeping this additional orientation in mind, I have added a column called "personalization" to our original chart. This expanded
version can be found on the next page.

Teaching Texts: Chart Two				
What is the text?	Shakespeare, Sonnet 73 ("That Time of Year")	Shakespeare, *The Merchant of Venice*	Stevens, "The Snow Man"	Jones, "The edge"
Orientation shorthand	Literary Criticism ("New Criticism")	Historical, contextual, biographical	Personal reader-response	Personalization
What is the orientation?	The text stands on its own. We learn "how the poem means" (its formal structures). We analyze its meaning in the light of its language and form.	Understanding the play requires knowing how it would have been understood in Shakespeare's time. We use "external" tools = anthropology, historical methods. Analysis of texts.	We explore the reader's experience qua reader. Reactions, reflections on methods by which text affects reader.	Literature is related to personal meaning. We learn who we are from reading others.
What is the "warrant" (for orientation)? E.g., specific scholarly resources behind it?	"New criticism" E.g., T. S. Eliot, John Crowe Ransom, Cleanth Brooks, John Ciardi	Cultural studies; literary history E.g., James Shapiro	Reader-response criticism E.g., Stanley Fish	Real-life practice ("wisdom of practice" à la Lee Shulman, Pamela Grossman)
What is the point (of lesson)?	Learning sonnet structure; investigating: Are formal structures aesthetic or semantic? Exploring the "argument" of the poem.	Viewing "pound of flesh" issue in the light of Shakespeare's time. How do sources of the period teach us about the play? Conversely, how does the play teach us about the period?	Each of us knows the poem in our own way. We explore the way the poem affects us (as a way of discovering its meanings).	The poem is essentially mysterious. We learn about ourselves and others as we study the poem.
What are the strategies (of the lesson)?	Analyze structures individually and in groups via writing and conversation. Compare to other poem ("Composed upon Westminster Bridge"). Questions and discussion led by teacher.	Examine and analyze source materials with presentation by teacher. Use original documents where possible.	Writing reactions. Importance of self-reflection. Opportunity to share with others in groups or pairs.	Writing reactions. Importance of self-reflection. Opportunity to share with others in groups or pairs.

Our main concern, of course, is with the teaching of Jewish texts, and while the chart on the previous page obviously evolves out of English literature, I would like to turn now to the ways that the approach to orientations that we have been exploring might be relevant to teaching the Bible as well.

Orientations for Teaching Bible

How might we begin to apply in a specific way the idea of orientations to the teaching of Bible? If at the outset we choose to take our point of authority, our "warrant," as being rooted in the world of the university, we find no simple answer to the question, What are the appropriate orientations for Bible teaching? Such orientations need to be rooted in the approaches to the study of Bible evidenced in the university, and the contemporary academic landscape is dotted with various methods of biblical scholarship, each of which might serve as a starting point for a pedagogy of Bible. In the words of one scholar:

> As recently as two decades ago, there was a consensus among scholars about using a fairly limited number of critical methods for the study of Bible, but today the spectrum of methods employed has enlarged dramatically. . . . How these different methods of biblical inquiry are to be related logically and procedurally has become a major intellectual challenge that will require a comprehensive frame of reference not readily at hand.[14]

These words, written by Gottwald in 1985, are even more true today where the modes of biblical criticism encompass a variety of approaches even more varied than those of almost two decades ago.[15]

Certainly, it is not the task of this chapter to attempt the synthesis of methods advocated by Gottwald above, or even to present a comprehensive catalog of such methods. Whether one uses Gottwald's own "angles of vision," Edward L. Greenstein's contrast of "synchronic" and "diachronic"[16] approaches to text, or the various attempts to organize contemporary literary approaches,[17] the task is a large one and beyond the scope of our project here. By way of illustration, one need only consider that even within the "literary" mode alone, we could begin with examples of classic "source criticism" and "form criticism," and continue all the way through present-day feminist, psychoanalytic, or political criticism, and many others as well. "Historical" approaches to the Bible also vary widely. In this area, for example, feminist works such as Meyers's *Discovering Eve* stand side by side with older approaches such as Noth's *The Old Testament World*,[18] with a great range in between.

What I wish to do here instead is to take a stance appropriate to an educational perspective: namely, to consider what methods of biblical research might fruitfully serve as a basis for pedagogy—indeed, what methods often do serve such a purpose. Organizing the approaches along the lines of the way we looked at orientations toward the teaching of literature earlier in this chapter, we can get a picture of some possible ways of thinking about the teaching of Bible. Following upon that discussion, I wish to turn to other approaches to the teaching of Bible, orientations that are less likely to be associated with the university and have their roots in the "wisdom of practice" of teachers and in various ideological or philosophical stances unrelated to the "scientific" study of the Bible. Ultimately, a "map" of various orientations to teaching Bible should begin to emerge.

Three Bible Teachers

Let us imagine, once again, different teachers: this time, teachers of Bible. How might they orient themselves vis-à-vis their subject matter? How might they prepare lessons for students—either adults or children? What grounds their educational thinking and pedagogic approaches?

We'll begin with David, who became interested in the Bible while spending his junior year of college in Israel. He was profoundly touched by the connection of the landscape of the Bible to the land he was literally walking on. He delighted in visiting archaeological sites, began reading books about the ancient Near East, and started to view the Bible as a living repository of the history of his people. The *realia,* the ancient cultures and languages, and the laws of ancient Israel and their comparison with neighboring laws and practices fascinated him. When David returned from Israel, he began to take religion courses at his university and found that most of his professors were similarly oriented in their approach to Bible. He poured over copies of the magazine *Biblical Archaeology Review* and even began to study Ugaritic, one of the ancient Semitic languages so important in biblical research.

In preparing his teaching, David found commentaries such as the Anchor Bible and the Jewish Publication Society Commentary on the Torah to be very useful.[19] For a class he was teaching at his local synagogue, David turned to one of the most popular and influential works about the Bible, Nahum Sarna's *Understanding Genesis.* Originally published by the Jewish Theological Seminary's Melton Research Center in 1966, Sarna's book was one of the first to bring "to the general reader a body of essential knowledge, the distillation and integration of the results of specialized research in many varied disciplines that shed light upon the biblical text."[20]

David wishes to show his students the world of biblical people, what they believed and felt, how they lived, and what they valued. He also admires Sarna's statement that "we have emphasized in this book the importance of difference, and have been at pains to delineate those areas in which Israel parted company with its neighbors."[21] Lessons comparing the Bible's Creation story with the creation myths of other ancient cultures were something that David was able to bring to his class.

David is now preparing to teach the Joseph story. Looking in *Understanding Genesis,* he notes Sarna's explanations of the text: the "coat of many colors," David learns, was "a token of special favor and perhaps, too, of luxury and lordship";[22] David sees the meaning of Joseph's dreams "against the background of the times";[23] he reads about the situation of slavery in ancient Egypt;[24] and he explores the comparison of the attempted seduction of Joseph in Genesis 39 to the "Tale of Two Brothers" (an ancient story).[25] All the data that David draws from Sarna's book allow David to focus and enrich the lessons he prepares for his students.

Let us imagine, now, a different case. Sarah was a literature major in college. Like some of the teachers studied by Pamela Grossman, Sarah cares about the close reading of literary works and sees her role as helping to guide students along that path of careful textual analysis. The literary critical approaches to fiction and poetry that she learned in college have influenced her thinking and beliefs about being a Bible teacher. But when she began to examine "literary" approaches to the study of Bible, she was astonished to find that most of the works that she consulted took a completely different view of the word "literary." In the words of Kenneth Gros Louis, "What has been called 'literary criticism' of the Bible is not the kind of literary criticism teachers of literature do. In fact, the biblical scholar's definition of 'literary criticism' is virtually the opposite of the literary critic's."[26] Sarah, however, has come upon Robert Alter's *The Art of Biblical Narrative,* and Alter's approach

was exactly what she was looking for. Here she read an approach toward "literary analysis," by which the author meant:

> the manifold varieties of minutely discriminating attention to the
> artful use of language, to the shifting play of ideas, conventions,
> tone, sound, imagery, syntax, narrative viewpoint, compositional
> units, and much else; the kind of disciplined attention, in other
> words, which through a whole spectrum of critical approaches
> has illuminated, for example, the poetry of Dante, the plays of
> Shakespeare, the novels of Tolstoy.[27]

Sarah looks at Gros Louis's article and finds his set of "questions a literary critic considers in approaching a work of literature"[28] very much what
she wants her students to consider in her classes: questions about the literary structure, style, tone, and characters' motivations, among others. An
article by Joel Rosenberg[29] helps her understand the particular features of
biblical narrative, and she wishes to help her students recognize these features and how they function in conveying the story's meaning.

Unlike David, Sarah is not particularly interested in the ancient
Near East and the historical background to the Bible. Using a term from
Alter, Sarah characterizes the approach that her fellow teacher David
admires as being "excavative" (she would say "merely excavative!");
that is, "either literally, with the archaeologist's spade and reference to
its findings, or with a variety of analytic tools intended to uncover the
original meanings of biblical words, the life situations in which specific
texts were used, the sundry sources from which longer texts were as-
sembled."[30] She, in contrast, wants her students to "read the text as it
is," as she likes to put it, not as it may have been understood in ancient
times. In the mode of the New Critics, Sarah wants the text "treated as
a privileged object that should be considered predominantly in its own
terms with contextual factors being assigned a minor role."[31]

Like David, Sarah is preparing to teach a unit on the Joseph stories
in Genesis, and she finds Alter's reading of the text particularly helpful.
His suggestion about the literary artistry of the tale will help guide the
way Sarah structures her lessons. In his reading of Genesis 42, Alter
points out the following, for example:

> The narrator, as we have noted, began the episode by emphati-
> cally and symmetrically stating Joseph's knowledge and the
> brothers' ignorance. Now through all this dialogue, he studiously

refrains from comment, allowing the dynamics of the relationship between Joseph and his brothers to be revealed solely through their words, and leaving us to wonder in particular about Joseph's precise motives. Whatever those may be, the alertness to analogy to which biblical narrative should have accustomed us ought to make us see that Joseph perpetrates on the brothers first a reversal, then a repetition, of what they did to him.[32]

This passage from Alter's analysis helps Sarah envision what she wants to concentrate on, what worksheets she might design for individualized learning, and what focusing questions she will ask in the whole-class discussions. Her goal is to prepare readers as interesting, involved, and insightful as Alter and the other newer interpreters of Bible whom she has subsequently discovered.[33]

Another teacher, Jill, is also interested in literary readings of biblical texts, but she is less under the influence of the classic "New Critics" and their disciples (as Sarah was) and more drawn to the reader-response writers. Her teachers in college were devotees of various reader-response approaches, and Jill herself was influenced by Stanley Fish's statement that the "concept [of this kind of criticism] is simply the rigorous and disinterested asking of the question, what does this word, phrase, sentence, paragraph, chapter, novel, play, poem, do? . . . The basis of the method is a consideration of the temporal flow of the reading experience, and it is assumed that the reader responds in terms of that flow and not to the whole utterance."[34] Like Sarah, Jill wants her students to become close readers of text, but she wants them to pay particular attention to the workings of the text on them, individually, as readers.

Jill also is preparing to teach the Joseph stories and has been influenced by an interpretation of the opening of the narrative written by the Bible scholar Edward L. Greenstein. As he explains his approach:

In my view it is the proper role of literary study to enable the reader to experience the text thoroughly—not to *explain* the text, but to *expose* it. Taking a cue from Martin Buber, the reader must experience the text not as an objectified "It" to be analyzed, but as a subjectified "Thou" to be encountered.[35]

For Jill, Greenstein's approach to the "confusion" and ambiguity in the text over who exactly sells Joseph to whom in Genesis 37 is a guide to the way that she will help her students become "encounterers" of the

Bible. The scholar speaks for her own aspirations when he says: "It behooves the student of biblical literature to acquire a method for reading biblical narratives *as they are told* [emphasis his], or as they 'tell themselves.'"[36]

In David, Sarah, and Jill, we have exemplars of teachers whose approach to Bible parallels, *mutatis mutandis,* the three approaches to text that Pamela Grossman described in her examination of literature teachers: the historical or contextual approach; the classic modernist literary analysis; and postmodern reader-response criticism. Earlier in this chapter, I exemplified these approaches in three different English literature lessons, summarized in Chart One above. As the reader will recall, upon examination of our original chart, I added a fourth category, "personalization," even though its academic "authority" is less fully developed than the other three approaches. How personalization relates to issues of Jewish education I will explore later in this chapter.

Let us for the time being stay with our three approaches to text and consider the specific issue of Bible as a subject area for teaching.[37] What other approaches to the teaching of Bible should we consider beyond the three exemplified above? One obvious candidate is the study of Bible in the light of its classic Jewish commentaries. Here we see a place in which Jewish education clearly differs from the approach to the study of literature found in general education. For even in universities (and certainly not in secondary schools), it is rare indeed to see the study of literary *criticism* (i.e., interpretive "commentaries" on Shakespeare or George Eliot or T. S. Eliot) go hand in hand with the study of these core texts.[38] One thinker, Robert Scholes, has indeed argued that introducing university students to literary criticism is an important activity. It is, according to Scholes, one of the ways that we can teach people how to interpret texts: namely, by showing them how others have done it. "The point of teaching interpretation," he argues,

> is not to usurp the interpreter's role but to explain the rules of the interpretive game. . . . These rules are common to all within the academic institution, as the rules of chess are common to all chess players. Therefore, we must teach the rules, and we must also teach the principles and procedures that lead to strong interpretive positions. . . . In literary study, it means that interpretations should be read and studied along with the texts they interpret—not every time or all the time, but enough so that students can see how it is done.[39]

Scholes's suggestion is an unusual one, though it has a good deal of pedagogic logic, but his approach differs radically from what I have mentioned as good classic Jewish pedagogy—using commentaries when studying the Bible. Scholes is arguing for the use of commentaries as heuristic models—if we read Stanley Fish, say, interpreting a George Herbert poem, it will help the student learn the skills of interpretation. We apprentice our students (and ourselves) to the masters of the trade. But the use of classic commentaries in Jewish education emanates from another reason entirely—Judaism views this literature of commentary as also being part of Torah.[40] It goes hand in hand with the Bible because it represents authentic, authoritative understanding of the Bible. These commentaries represent the tradition of how "we" (that is, Jewish sages throughout the ages) understand Torah.[41]

Of course, one of the pleasures of the Jewish interpretive literature is that there is no one authoritative understanding of the text, going back at least to the time of the classical midrashim. There is a wide range of views found within the tradition. As one scholar has put it, "the characteristic of early rabbinic commentary that is most distinctive . . . [is] its multiplicity of interpretations."[42] Educationally, it is possible for the teacher to view this range of interpretations as something to be embraced or something to be avoided. That is, a teacher may choose to limit the students' access to this range by presenting the tradition as if there is only one authoritative view (this is typical of the way Rashi, the great medieval commentator, is used in some Orthodox schools). Others see presenting divergent views within the tradition as one of the goals of learning itself. Perhaps the most well-known exponent of the latter approach is the late professor Nehama Leibowitz, who, over the course of decades, focused on classic biblical commentaries in both her classes and her numerous writings.[43]

Although Nehama Leibowitz lived and worked around the world of universities in Israel, her approach to teaching Bible was only partially located in the university approach to the discipline. The "warrant" for Nehama Leibowitz's approach was much less the academy's method of biblical research than it was a classic Jewish religious perspective to approaching the text through its commentaries. Leibowitz was not a historian who focused on the historical or intellectual context of the commentator, as university scholars might conventionally do. She was interested in the commentator as a window into the Bible itself or into the way we should understand the Bible.[44]

It is no accident that her studies of biblical works bear the subtitle "in the context of ancient and modern Jewish Bible commentary,"[45] indicating her focus on the Bible itself rather than on the history of biblical interpretation. As Leibowitz once noted:

> I learned to read *Tanakh* from our great medieval commentators, Rashi, Ramban and Rashbam and from their successors who, to a certain extent, followed in their footsteps. . . . [The thing that they and their successors had in common is] something which I regard as very important to teach: the seriousness with which they relate to the written word, to every word; not only to the big word filled with deep significance and loaded with religious-ideological explosiveness.[46]

Here we see Leibowitz's commitment to a "close reading" of the biblical text—in a sense, the place where traditional reading and modern literary criticism appear to meet. Her approach emanates directly out of the oldest notions of Jewish Bible interpretation, something that James Kugel has characterized as "the doctrine of 'omnisignificance,' whereby nothing in Scripture is said in vain or for rhetorical flourish: every detail is important, everything is intended to impart some teaching."[47] It is important to add that despite the shared method of close reading, modern literary criticism and traditional biblical interpretation are at heart quite different enterprises, based on different foundational assumptions and beliefs about the text.[48]

A typical example of Leibowitz's method is found in her approach to the early part of the Joseph story. (It should be said that Leibowitz offers a number of different "studies" for this story. I am only choosing one.) Leibowitz explores the puzzling section in Gen. 37:28 in which Joseph is sold into slavery either by "Midianites" or "Ishmaelites," or, as the text says later, by "Medanites." Her method is to look at the understandings of this confusing narrative by a variety of medieval commentators, with reference back to the midrashic literature and forward to more modern, though nonetheless traditional, commentators such as Samson Raphael Hirsch and Benno Jacob. Where Sarna, using a historical/contextual approach, will point out that the "variation may well be due to an interweaving of different traditions"[49] and Greenstein (see n. 35 above) will look at the effect on the reader of the textual ambiguity, Leibowitz is interested in the way that traditional commentators dealt with the problem and what they were expressing about the Bible through their solutions.

With a careful eye to the implications behind each of the commentator's views, Leibowitz asks, in typical fashion: "But the main question is how does this new interpretation affect the significance of the story as a whole?"[50] This question stands behind much of her work and explains a good deal of why her writing is so attractive to educators—Leibowitz aims immediately for the significance of the text. One can easily imagine a teacher taking Leibowitz's chapter, photocopying the various excerpts from the commentators, and basing his or her lesson around an exploration of these texts. Even the questions that Leibowitz appends to each "study" are well suited for a teacher's use.

We could term Leibowitz's orientation the "*parshanut*" or "Jewish interpretive" approach, and with her example, we have moved ever so slightly outside the warrant of the academy into other educational justifications for teaching practice. Hers stems from a combination of her own sense of the appropriate ways that the Bible has been interpreted according to Jewish tradition and, I imagine, her vision of what is most appropriate for educational settings. Over her career, there have been without doubt many teachers who saw in Leibowitz's approach something that resonated with their own sense of what the "best" way to teach Bible is, even if that approach was not rooted directly in what is generally done in universities.

Our investigation of Leibowitz has led us, then, to another question: For the teacher, where precisely does the "authority" of any discipline reside? For teachers (and scholars) in general education, the answer is obvious. The overarching criterion of authority is the world of the university and its culture, rules, and modes of discourse. That is, while there may be different "substantive structures" (as Schwab would put it)[51] represented by, let's say, the approach of social historians versus the approach of intellectual historians, nonetheless, the rules of argument, inquiry, and acceptable analysis will be shared by all, even if the conclusions are different in the extreme. For a professor like Schwab sitting at the University of Chicago, such an assumption seems almost tautological—as it would to most educators working within the central educational institutions in the Western world. Thus, one educational scholar remarks:

The "form of knowledge" approach to history is concerned, as far as may be possible, to teach children the rules of the game historians play. Admittedly, the subject does not lack for controversy, and many historians disagree on important points of principle; but these debates presuppose a universe of discourse and it is the rules and mores of this universe that the adolescent must at least begin to penetrate.[52]

But if we turn to Jewish education, we quickly see that the authority of the discipline may reside in multiple locations, not all of which are within the university. In the world of the ultraorthodox yeshiva, for example, the rules of discourse are completely different, as is the definition of an acceptable "syntactical" structure,[53] to use Schwab's term. If in the university, the tools of archaeology, comparative philology, anthropology, and historical documentation are all basic and acceptable means of exploring the biblical text, in the yeshiva these are completely irrelevant or forbidden.[54] The substantive structures are, in the same manner, completely different as well. For the yeshiva teacher, the meaning of the text is what the classical commentators reveal it to be. More significantly, the Bible is God's word, not a human document, and even the way university scholars might talk about the genres and subgenres of the Bible—narrative, law, prophecy, and so on—is unimaginable. The Bible, for the yeshiva teacher, is not a collection of different types of literature; it is a seamless whole.

Schwab's description of substantive structures does not take into account the possibility that there may be modes of discourse that do not fit the basic rules of university life. But in the realm of Jewish religious education, we must accept the reality of multiple approaches to the discipline, some of which are governed by the rules of university discourse, and others of which will be quite different[55]—so different, in fact, that even the word "discipline" is outside of realm of discourse.

In many ways, my argument here resembles the notion of "interpretive communities" of textual interpretation, as it appears in the work of the literary critic Stanley Fish. That is, the way we read texts—and, in our case, the way we teach texts—is deeply connected to the community to which we belong. Fish claims that the "interpretive strategies" employed by individual readers "exist prior to the act of reading and therefore determine the shape of what is read rather than, as is usually assumed, the other way around."[56] I am hesitant to go quite as far as Fish does and claim that "since the thoughts an individual can think and the mental operations he can perform have their source in some or other interpretive community, he is as much the product of that community (acting as an extension of it) as the meanings it enables him to produce."[57] But I do believe that the idea of interpretive communities allows us to see how related, in Schwab's language, the "commonplace" of subject matter is to that of milieu. We live in communities that help us understand texts, what we want to accomplish when we teach them, where we see ourselves, and where we see our students and their futures.

Thus, once again we return to the idea of goals and outcomes. The goals of an individual teacher, surely related to the community in which he or she is located (though not, I believe, entirely determined by it), will profoundly influence how he or she teaches, even down to the very definition of the discipline itself. What, for example, are the rules of textual interpretation that are "allowed" or encouraged? Is Rashi—representing here traditional exegesis—the source of "truth" for a teacher, or is it the academic "truth" of the modern Anchor Bible commentary?

Why might a teacher choose to model his or her teaching on Leibowitz's approach rather than a more typical university orientation? Any particular teacher's orientations toward teaching a text (or indeed, toward any pedagogic situation, such as teaching mathematics) emanate, it appears, from a combination of at least three sources: a) the particular personality and temperament of the teacher him- or herself;[58] b) the available "authoritative" models of one's milieu or culture (i.e., one's "interpretive community"); and c) the "wisdom of practice," as it has been experienced by the teacher, either in his or her own career or in knowing about the practices of other teachers. Some of those "other teachers" may be colleagues, others may be the teachers of one's own youth,[59] and still others may transmit their "wisdom" through books and articles. The teacher in this view "is not only a master of procedure but also of content and rationale . . . capable of explaining why something is done."[60] Teachers, then, have their own views about what should be done in the classroom, based on their sense not merely of "what works" but also of what is "worth" doing.

Earlier in this chapter, I raised "wisdom of practice" as a possible warrant for the personalization orientation. It may also serve as a source for other orientations as well. But how might wisdom of practice be investigated? Aside from observing teachers at work in classrooms or interviewing them, perhaps the best way to understand wisdom of practice is to look at the curriculum materials actually used by teachers as an indication of the way they may approach their particular subjects. Certainly, it is true that decisions about the books that a class uses are not entirely in the hands of teachers alone. But the popularity of certain books—and the way that those books attempt to reflect the actual practices of teachers—makes looking at textbooks a valuable and instructive exercise.[61] As Ball and Cohen note:

Unlike frameworks, objectives, assessments, and other mecha-
nisms that seek to guide curriculum, instructional materials are
concrete and daily. They are the stuff of lessons and units, of
what teachers and students do. That centrality affords curricular materials a uniquely intimate connection to teaching.[62]

If we turn to one popular example, an orientation to the teaching of
Bible different from what we have seen up to now becomes apparent. *A
Child's Bible,* by Seymour Rossel, aims to look at the narratives in the
Bible as a means of instructing us today in the way we should behave.
"The people in the stories," we read in the introduction for the student,
"are always a lot like us. So the stories help us learn how we should
live, what we should do, and how we should behave."[63] The aim is to
see "what [the stories] mean to us today," and in order to do so, students should ask themselves: " 'What truth is this story teaching me?'
'What does this story say that I should do?' 'How does this story say
that I should behave?' "[64]

We see the method exemplified in the textbook's explanation of various biblical tales. Thus, in its discussion of the Tower of Babel story
(under the headline "What does it mean?"), the student reads:

> The builders on the tower looked down and saw everything
> below getting smaller and smaller. It made them feel stronger
> and more important than the people below. They began to think
> that they were as mighty as God.
>
> You do not have to be on top of a tall tower to look down on
> other people. You can just say or think that a person is some-
> one to "look down on," someone less important than you.
>
> But really, God makes each of us special, so every person is im-
> portant. Every person has something special to offer the world.
> "Looking down" on people is always a mistake. It's like "mak-
> ing war with God."[65]

To return to our earlier example of teaching the Joseph story, we see in *A
Child's Bible* a discussion that includes, under "What does it mean?":
"Your dreams teach you things you need to know. Even a bad dream can
help you grow stronger."[66] And under "What does it teach?" (the distinction between this and "What does it mean?" is not entirely clear to me):

Joseph heard Pharaoh say that there were two dreams. But he listened very carefully. And that is how he discovered that both were really one and the same dream. If you want to help people by listening to them, you must first listen to their words. But then you must also try to hear what their words mean. Joseph was a good listener.[67]

The biblical stories, according to this view, are important for the moral lessons that they communicate. Unlike the academic literary method— and the pedagogic approach that emanates from it—which aims at opening up the complexity, indeed, the ambiguity, of the biblical narrative, *A Child's Bible* is oriented toward simplifying the biblical tale into a specific "teaching," as Rossel puts it in his introduction. Contrast this with Alter's comment that "an essential aim of the innovative technique of fiction worked out by the ancient Hebrew writers was to produce a certain indeterminancy of meaning, especially in regard to motive, moral character, and psychology."[68] Perhaps for this reason, *A Child's Bible* does not use the actual biblical text itself (filled with the many ambiguities that writers such as Alter, Greenstein, Rosenberg, and others delight in pointing out), but rather retells the stories, leaving out the inconvenient complexities of the original and adding clarifying points on its own.[69]

The underlying assumption of this approach is that the Bible communicates clear lessons, and the details of the narratives are to be understood as pointing us in the way of good moral behavior. Educationally, *A Child's Bible* has the advantage of being accessible to children and clear about its outcomes. The Bible, in these lessons, has something to tell us, and in each case we will be able to define what that something (to be fair, it is "somethings," in the plural) is. Children can take home these messages and feel that the Bible speaks to them.

Alter and others would no doubt argue that such an educational approach sends a not-so-hidden message that the Bible is simple, perhaps even simplistic. The Bible becomes a kind of Jewish Aesop's Fables. That, those critics would assert, is an unfortunate message to communicate to children: not only is it an inaccurate portrayal of the Bible, but it works to the detriment of Jewish education in the long run. The Bible will be understood as far less sophisticated than other literatures that children will encounter, and therefore they will always think of it as a childish thing.[70]

In the approach of *A Child's Bible*, we can see quite clearly one attempt to personalize the experience of learning Bible. But I think it differs significantly from the example of personalization cited earlier in this chapter in the description of the lesson teaching the poem "The edge." *A Child's Bible* represents personalization with a moral tone. The stories are meant to teach us *lessons*. Because of that, I would suggest that we distinguish this orientation as a "didactic" or "moralistic" approach to Bible. Although *A Child's Bible* is aimed at the more liberal sector within Jewish religious practice, ironically, it resembles approaches seen in more traditional communities, such as found in the textbooks called *Gateway to Torah*.[71]

Although the moralistic approach focuses on finding the meanings of the biblical text, it differs from the literary orientation in at least two ways. First, as I mentioned above, it eschews close reading of text and its consequent emphasis on the nuance and specific vocabulary and tone of the biblical text, replacing close reading with an expanded retelling of the narrative. Second, it aims to extract a kind of specific message from the text. A literary method is never about uncovering a message to learn, though people may certainly learn such messages from their reading of texts. We don't expect a person to read *Hamlet* and say that the moral of the story is "don't be wishy-washy about making decisions" or "don't listen to ghosts when they give you missions." Indeed, these comical attempts to sum up the play indicate exactly the nature of the problem: great literary works are admired for their complexity, their ability to mirror the complexity of life itself, perhaps, and not because we can learn a simple lesson from them. Hence, no one puts Oedipus and Aesop's fable of "The Fox and Grapes" at the same level of literary accomplishment. In the same spirit, Rosenberg speaks about the nature of the biblical narrative:

> [I]t is impossible to distill *the* message of biblical narrative. Attempts to generalize yield only moral and theological truisms that do violence to the Bible's special way of talking. Biblical narrative rarely moralizes. It explores moral questions, to be sure, but it is in the wit and nuance of the specific moment that one is to find the narrative's intelligence most concentrated. This intelligence steadfastly withholds itself from stating "messages." It allows its messages to arise from silences in the narrative. In a sense, it is *weighing* messages, in that discordant voices in the tradition are allowed silently to clash, even as the narrative plunges inexorably forward.[72]

It is important to note that the classic New Critical literary approach does not aim at confronting the issue of the personal meaning of the text in the life of the reader. The teacher who uses a literary orientation needs to understand that although the student may uncover many meanings in the biblical text, none need address his or her own experience or life. The teacher with a literary orientation might never ask the student, "Well, what does this mean to you?" For that, we need to turn to another orientation, that which earlier in this chapter I called "personalization."

Personalization and Bible Teaching

Personalization suggests another route when we apply the category to Bible teaching, different from the literary on the one hand, but different from the moralistic on the other. In the twentieth century, perhaps the most powerful representation of this approach to the Bible comes from Martin Buber. In his essay "The Man of Today and the Jewish Bible," Buber tries to find a way to encounter the Bible directly in our lives.[73] Too often, Buber says, people today view the Bible in a distant, "abstract" way with "an interest connected with the history of religion or civilization, or an aesthetic interest, or the like—at any rate it is an interest that springs from the detached spirit"[74] of contemporary life. We picture Buber watching our friend David teach, as David uses his "contextual" orientation; we imagine Buber observing Sarah's lessons as she explores the "aesthetic" of the biblical text. Neither satisfies Buber; both seem too safe, neither "confronts . . . life with the Word."[75] Instead, Buber argues for another course. The "man of today," Buber says,

> can open up to this book and let its rays strike him where they will. . . . He can absorb the Bible with all his strength, and wait to see what will happen to him. . . . .
>
> He must yield to it, withhold nothing of his being, and let whatever will occur between himself and it. He does not know which of its sayings and images will overwhelm him and mold him, from where the spirit will ferment and enter into him. . . . But he holds himself open.[76]

This remarkable passage could well serve as the defining motto of personalization in regard to reading and teaching the Bible. Certainly, it is not easy to picture what it would mean to translate it to an educational orientation, a way of *teaching*. But there have been attempts at *reading* the Bible in this way that might offer a teacher some guidance, in the same way that Sarna helps a teacher using a historical approach and Leibowitz is an aid to teachers using a Jewish interpretive approach.

In looking at such personalist readings of the Bible, however, we will also realize that even within personalization we can delineate a variety of approaches. One might be called "personalization with a psychological perspective." As one recent writer has put it, "with every story we study, we learn not only about what we are reading, but also about ourselves. In deciphering a text, we bring to the fore elements of our own being of which we may not always be conscious. We respond to our own questions and dilemmas."[77] Reading biblical narratives "can serve as vehicles of insight into our own personalities as well as the dynamic tensions within our own families."[78] The study of these texts serves a healing function—they can help our own "search for wholeness."[79]

Other personalist approaches suggest more of a political agenda; still others take a more religious/spiritual approach. All personalist approaches, however, share a common goal: to find the links between a person's life and the biblical text.[80]

The "Big Ideas" of the Bible

Looking once again at various curriculum materials produced for the teaching of Bible, we can see another orientation, one that differs from the personalist modes discussed above, but that ultimately tries to find its own way into the issue of personal meaning and the Bible. This is seen in the Bible curriculum of the Melton Research Center, which was mentioned earlier in this chapter. To begin with, we can see that the Melton materials were influenced by the contextual orientation as well as by the literary approach. Indeed, a comparison between Sarna's *Understanding Genesis* (as we said earlier, this book was originally written for Melton) and the original Melton teacher's guide by Leonard Gardner[81] shows the way that Gardner's work—very early on in the history of the Melton Research Center—introduced literary approaches and reduced the amount of ancient Near Eastern comparisons that had appeared in Sarna's work.[82]

Gardner's writing is clearly aimed at the classroom teacher, and it appears that he (or perhaps better, he and the leadership of the Melton Center at that time) believed that a literary approach was more appropriate for classroom use. One need only compare Sarna's approach to the Joseph story with Gardner's to see the difference. In later years, the revised Melton curriculum materials written by Ruth Zielenziger lean even more heavily toward a literary orientation.[83]

But it would be inaccurate to term the Melton orientation as "literary," or only literary. Instead of a concern for the literary features of the text alone, the lessons in the curriculum might be characterized as an "ideational" approach; that is, its primary focus is on answering the question, What are the "big ideas" that the Bible is expressing? Or perhaps better, one could say, What are the values of the Bible? As Gardner put it:

> There are two kinds of activities at which the lesson plans aim. The first is an analysis of the structure of the text. This requires a close reading of the text and a search for the particular devices which are employed: repetition, opening and closing statements; turning points or reversals. . . .
>
> The second kind of classroom activity at which we aim is to take each of the Bible stories as a metaphor which communicates an important idea. Thus in our analysis of the text, we search for the idea in its metaphorical expression. Once discovered, we work to make the idea clear in a more literal mode and to apply it to our own experience.[84]

From this passage, we see that although there is interest in the literary features of the text, the primary goal is to uncover the "idea in its metaphorical expression," to see the major moral and theological insights or ideas of the Bible.[85] Examples of "big ideas" and values found in the curriculum are "the basic belief in the essential goodness of the universe" that we learn from the Creation story and "the endowment of man with moral autonomy and the stress upon the human aspect of evil" that we learn from the Cain and Abel story.[86]

Though it uses close reading of the text, the Melton approach differs from the "literary" approach of Robert Alter and others because it seeks to extract a kind of message from the text.[87] That message, however, is not framed in the mode of a moralistic or didactic reading, but rather represents an account of the philosophical underpinnings of various biblical texts.

A Call to Action

But the Melton materials blend in another orientation as well, one that we have not yet examined: the idea that learning Torah is intended to move people toward *action*. The particular "action" in this case is represented in what Gardner, in the passage above, calls the need "to apply" biblical ideas "to our own experience." That call to action is what the Melton writers defined as "character education," and the curriculum viewed this as the ultimate goal of Bible study.

How was character education supposed to occur? The most serious attempt to answer that question was attempted by Burton Cohen and Joseph Schwab in an article called "Practical Logic: Problems of Ethical Decision."[88] In this article, the authors argue that although "emotional factors may play a primary role in the development of character it seems likely that the role of intellect will not be an insignificant one."[89] By arguing for the role of "advancing the student's character development through his intellect,"[90] the authors saw an opportunity to relate the normal work of schools (learning of subject matter) to questions of character and ethical development of individuals, a match that made a great deal of sense in the realm of Jewish education, where intellectual activities are framed by a larger religious agenda.

The method to accomplish this was through a set of exercises that related the ethical principles learned in studying Genesis to "life situations" through an approach that the authors called "practical logic."[91] Practical logic is a sophisticated method of ethical reasoning, based around the notion that applying an ethical precept to a particular life situation is not a simple matter of learning a moral aphorism or idea and then behaving in the manner expected by this principle. Rather, the application of biblical "lessons" to life involves a host of challenges to the individual, including (among the five "problems" discussed in the article): "the difficulty of identifying which ethical principle is applicable to a particular set of circumstances"[92] and the fact that "a given concrete situation evokes from . . . [a person's] catalogue of ethical precepts not one, but two or more apparently equally valid but apparently irreconcilable principles."[93]

The ethical challenges that the authors suggest in their exercises are imaginative attempts to move students toward careful consideration of the various difficulties involved in applying ethical principles. Most important, practical logic allows students to see the way that the things they are learning in their Bible classes are directly relevant to contemporary life. Hence, the examples chosen by the authors for the exercises include discussions of the biblical Creation story, the story of Noah, and the narrative of the destruction of Sodom and Gomorrah as a means of looking at contemporary issues such as ecology, honesty in government, and civil rights in the American South (of the early 1960s), among others.

Practical logic was an approach to dealing with the "relevance" of the Bible in modes far more subtle and thoughtful than the way that that term later came to be used in educational parlance. We can also see it as part of a much older tradition within Judaism about the purpose of studying Torah as a means to lead a person to action. Cohen and Schwab are arguing for the study of ethical principles to lead toward the ethical character development of individuals.

Classical Jewish sources, using their own terminology and values, saw the purpose of study as leading a person toward observing the mitzvot, the commandments.[94] Of course, within the Jewish tradition there is a great deal of debate about the ultimate purposes of studying Torah—is the activity an end in itself? Does it have a purely intellectual purpose, a spiritual purpose, or is it intended to lead us to performing the commandments? Clearly, there is a great deal of debate about these questions within the sources, but there is no doubt that one significant tradition—perhaps the dominant view—holds that there is a direct relationship between study and action.[95] When we learn Torah, we are moved toward doing; study is not merely an intellectual activity.

One sees this in obvious ways within the classical literature—particularly in the way that biblical prooftexts are brought to give authority to rabbinic statements about performing the commandments and even in the way that a genre of Jewish legal literature lists the 613 traditional commandments in the order in which they "appear" (via interpretation) in the Bible. The most famous of these is the anonymous medieval work called, interestingly, *Sefer hahinukh,* the Book of Education![96]

The "Map" for Teaching Bible

Let me try to summarize the discussion above with an outline of our map of orientations for teaching Bible. These are the various stances toward the biblical text that teachers may hold or choose to hold.

1. The Contextual Orientation: This approach aims at the meaning of the biblical texts *within its own times,* as best as we can determine it. It views the Bible as a record of an ancient civilization, and it hopes to make that world intelligible to students of today. This is the mode of Bible study that has most characterized the modern university, at least until quite recently. This orientation to teaching Bible has also been very influential in the secular school system in Israel, though much less so in the Diaspora. Building links to the ancient Land of Israel through the study of Bible (especially in the physical presence of the land itself) has been a primary goal of the public school in Israel.[97] It should be noted that the contextual approach includes a variety of dimensions, including the use of various tools that help locate the Bible in its historical setting. These might include source criticism (looking at the strands of tradition that come together to form the biblical text as we know it, that is, the "documentary hypothesis"), form criticism (looking at all the formal patterns within and among texts), comparative linguistics (understanding the language of the Bible through looking at other languages that are linguistically related), and archaeology, among others.

2. The Literary Criticism Orientation: This approach aims at literary readings of biblical texts, using the tools of modern criticism. There is a wide range of approaches possible within this domain, but most pay careful attention to the style, language, characters, themes, and forms of the biblical text. Such approaches are far more commonly used with biblical narratives and poetry than legal, prophetic, or wisdom-literature sections of the Bible.

3. The Reader-Response Orientation: This in some ways is a subset of the literary approach, but it differs significantly enough for me to separate it out here. What characterizes this style of teaching is that it focuses on the experience of the reader in encountering the text—what happens to the reader and how the text itself is structured to affect the reader are the concern here. Once again, this approach is far more commonly used with biblical narratives and poetry than legal, prophetic, or wisdom-literature sections of the Bible. Note that "personalization" (no. 6 below) also focuses very strongly on the reader's experience of the text. Pamela Grossman's use of the term "reader-response" encompasses both "reader-response" in its more technical, literary critical, sense and personalization.

4. Parshanut, the Jewish Interpretive Orientation: This approach is one of the traditional modes of teaching the Bible. The teacher is concerned with the way that various classical interpreters (Rashi, Nahmanides, Rashbam, etc.) understand the text. The goal, in general, is for students to become knowledgeable about these views. Nehama Leibowitz took this approach a step further and popularized the focus on seeing the contrasts among the interpreters and trying to determine what underlies these contrasting views.

5. Moralistic-Didactic Orientation: This approach aims at discerning the "message" (or messages) that specific biblical texts offer for our own lives. This approach may depend on the classical commentators, or it may offer independent analysis that would lead us to these lessons for today. A close reading of the biblical text itself is often irrelevant to the method, since the goal is to see the lesson behind the text, and for that a close concentration of the text itself may be unnecessary.

6. The Personalization Orientation: This approach also aims at the contemporary meaning of the biblical text but tends to do so in a less didactic and directive fashion than the approach above. These meanings may be characterized as psychologically oriented, politically oriented, or spiritually oriented. In all cases, the goal is to see the relationship between text and the life of today.

7. *The Ideational Orientation:* This approach essentially views the Bible as a kind of "philosophical" text in which are embedded certain key moral and theological ideas. The teacher is asking the question, What are the "big ideas" and values of the Bible? At times, such an approach can blend with the contextual approach, in that the key ideas of the Bible may be the ideas of its particular historical period. But in general, the approach is interested much more in the enduring and relevant ideas of the Bible throughout the ages (such as "human beings are created in the image of God") and how these ideas may be important for people today.

8. *The Bible Leads to Action Orientation:* Traditionally, this was the approach that saw the purpose of Bible study as leading to observing the mitzvot. In contemporary times, this approach has also led to a sophisticated orientation toward "character education."

Finally, there is one orientation to teaching that we did not deal with in the earlier sections of this chapter. Its elements are so elementary that it is easy to overlook, but despite its rote elements, it is important not to ignore this widespread teaching orientation, and I add it here:

9. *The Decoding, Translation, and Comprehension Orientation:* This is simply the basic comprehension of the text—decoding (i.e., pronouncing) the Hebrew, translating it from Hebrew, understanding the "facts," the characters' names, the plot details of stories, the nature of the laws, and the plain meaning of the words. Sometimes, it includes memorizing sections of the text or learning to sing the verses according to traditional cantillation notes. Such an approach represents, at its best, the vast comprehensive knowledge that students once were able to attain. At its worst, it can be mind-numbing and tedious.[98]

We can represent the elements of our map in the following chart:

Orientation	Key Element	Examples	Where Found?
The Contextual Orientation	Bible in the context of its own times	Academic research on Bible—historically oriented studies	Universities; secular schools in Israel
The Literary Criticism Orientation	Tools of modern literary criticism applied to the Bible	Academic research on Bible—literary critical studies; sometimes in textbooks	Universities; some (usually) non-Orthodox schools
The Reader-Response Orientation	Tools of postmodern literary criticism applied to the Bible	Academic research on Bible—literary critical studies; sometimes in textbooks	Universities; some (usually) non-Orthodox schools
Parshanut, the Jewish Interpretive Orientation	Exploration of classical commentators' understanding of Bible	Nehama Leibowitz as a model	Schools of various sorts, though mainly Orthodox; rarely in universities
Moralistic-Didactic Orientation	What is the moral lesson that the Bible teaches us?	Textbooks	Schools of various sorts, both Orthodox and non-Orthodox
The Personalization Orientation	How can the Bible speak to us—psychologically, politically, spiritually?	Usually not in curriculum materials—found in contemporary works on the Bible	Schools of various sorts
The Ideational Orientation	What are the "big ideas" of the Bible?	Melton curriculum as a model	Schools, mainly non-Orthodox
The Bible Leads to Action Orientation	Study leads us to performing commandments; ethical behavior	Found in textbooks of various sorts	Schools of various sorts
The Decoding, Translating, and Comprehension Orientation	Decoding the Hebrew, comprehending the basics	Found in older textbooks	All schools

Outlining the map is not the end of our task, for many questions remain about the use of this theoretical construct in practice. What are the practical implications of having such a map? In what way might it guide or influence Bible teachers or those responsible for working with teachers? How does the map of orientations relate to the question of a teacher's goals? In the next chapter, we will turn to these questions.

Notes

1. See, for example, Paul Fussell, *Poetic Meter and Poetic Form* (New York: Random House, 1979).
2. John Ciardi, *How Does a Poem Mean?* (Boston: Houghton Mifflin, 1959).
3. Quoted in James Shapiro, *Shakespeare and the Jews* (New York: Columbia University Press, 1996), p. 126.
4. Wallace Stevens, *Poems,* selected by Samuel French Morse (New York: Vintage, 1957), p. 23.
5. Richard Jones, *A Perfect Time* (Port Townsend, Wash.: Copper Canyon, 1994), pp. 76–77.
6. Terry Eagleton, *Literary Theory: An Introduction,* 2d ed. (Oxford: Blackwell, 1996), p. 74.
7. Jane P. Tompkins, ed., *Reader-Response Criticism: From Formalism to Post-Structuralism* (Baltimore: Johns Hopkins University Press, 1980), p. ix. Note also that there is no inherent contradiction between reader-response criticism and the "close reading" of the text associated with New Critics and like-minded educators. Indeed, reader-response, such as it is practiced by Fish and others, calls for a great sensitivity to the nuances of the text, which can only be attained by close readings. A good example is Stephen Booth's book *An Essay on Shakespeare's Sonnets* (New Haven: Yale University Press, 1969), in which the author states that his goal is "not to give a reading of the poems but to discover what in them or about them results in the reading experiences they evoke" (p. x). See, for instance, his comments on Sonnet 73 discussed in the first "model lesson" in this chapter (Booth, pp. 118–30).
8. See Stanley Fish, *Is There a Text in This Class?* (Cambridge: Harvard University Press, 1980).
9. Pamela L. Grossman, *The Making of a Teacher: Teacher Knowledge and Teacher Education* (New York: Teachers College Press, 1990), p. 88.
10. Ibid., p. 89.
11. See, for example, Nancy K. Miller, *Getting Personal: Feminist Occasions and Other Autobiographical Acts* (New York: Routledge, 1991); or Diane P. Freedman, Olivia Frey, and Francis Murphy Zauhar, *The Intimate Critique: Autobiographical Literary Criticism* (Durham, N.C.: Duke University Press, 1993). Or

the autobiographical works by critics such as Frank Lentricchia, *The Edge of Night* (New York: Random House, 1994); and Jane P. Tompkins, *A Life in School: What the Teacher Learned* (Reading, Mass.: Addison-Wesley, 1996).

12. Miller, *Getting Personal*, p. 1.

13. This is what Lee Shulman and others have called "the wisdom of practice." See Lee S. Shulman, "Those Who Understand: Knowledge Growth in Teaching," *Educational Researcher* 15, no. 2 (1986): 4–14.

14. Norman K. Gottwald, *The Hebrew Bible: A Socio-Literary Introduction* (Philadelphia: Fortress, 1985), p. 7.

15. See the comments of Edward L. Greenstein, "Biblical Studies in a State," in *The State of Jewish Studies*, ed. Shaye J. D. Cohen and Edward L. Greenstein (Detroit: Wayne State University Press, 1990). Also Greenstein's "The Torah as She Is Read," in his collection of essays, *Essays on Biblical Method and Translation* (Atlanta: Scholars Press, 1989).

16. Ibid.; see, in particular, pp. 32–38.

17. Such as those offered in *The New Literary Criticism and the Hebrew Bible*, ed. J. Cheryl Exum and David J. A. Clines (Sheffield, Eng.: Sheffield Academic Press, 1993). For an overview of various approaches, see Steven L. McKenzie and Stephen R. Haynes, eds., *To Each Its Own Meaning* (Louisville: Westminster John Knox, 1999). Also, Walter C. Kaiser and Moises Silva, *An Introduction to Biblical Hermeneutics: The Search for Meaning* (Grand Rapids, Mich.: Zondervan, 1994).

18. Carol Meyers, *Discovering Eve* (Oxford: Oxford University Press, 1988); Martin Noth, *The Old Testament World* (Philadelphia: Fortress, 1966).

19. The Anchor Bible series comprises many volumes, all published by Doubleday in New York, over the course of over three decades. The JPS (of Philadelphia) Torah Commentary appears in five volumes: Nahum M. Sarna on Genesis (1989), Sarna on Exodus (1991), Baruch A. Levine on Leviticus (1989), Jacob Milgrom on Numbers (1990), and Jeffrey H. Tigay on Deuteronomy (1996).

20. Nahum M. Sarna, *Understanding Genesis* (New York: Melton Research Center and Schocken, 1966), p. xxxiii.

21. Ibid., p. xxvii.

22. Ibid., p. 212.

23. Ibid.

24. Ibid., p. 213.

25. Ibid., pp. 214–15.

26. Kenneth R. R. Gros Louis, "Some Methodological Considerations," in *Literary Interpretations of Biblical Narratives*, ed. Kenneth R. R. Gros Louis with James S. Ackerman (Nashville: Abingdon, 1982), 2:14.

27. Robert Alter, *The Art of Biblical Narrative* (New York: Basic Books, 1981), pp. 12–13.

28. Gros Louis, "Some Methodological Considerations," p. 17. His "questions" appear on pp. 17–20.

29. Joel Rosenberg, "Biblical Narrative," in *Back to the Sources: Reading the Classic Jewish Texts,* ed. Barry W. Holtz (New York: Simon and Schuster / Summit, 1984), particularly pp. 37–62.

30. Alter, *The Art of Biblical Narrative,* p. 13.

31. K. M. Newton, *Interpreting the Text* (New York and London: Harvester Wheatsheaf, 1990), p. 174.

32. Alter, *The Art of Biblical Narrative,* pp. 165–66.

33. There are many works that a teacher like Sarah could turn to for help. Aside from the writers already mentioned in this chapter and just limiting the list to books in English, she would find the readings in the following of great pedagogic assistance: Michael Fishbane's discussion of both narrative and poetry in *Text and Texture* (New York: Schocken, 1979); Meir Sternberg's *The Poetics of Biblical Narrative* (Bloomington: Indiana University Press, 1985); George W. Savran's *Telling and Retelling: Quotation in Biblical Narrative* (Bloomington: Indiana University Press, 1988); Mieke Bal's *Lethal Love* (Bloomington: Indiana University Press, 1987); and Herbert Levine's readings of Psalms in his *Sing Unto God a New Song* (Bloomington: Indiana University Press, 1995). In addition, there is the marvelous translation of the Pentateuch in English, based on the Buber-Rosenzweig German version, done by the American scholar Everett Fox, with its excellent commentaries, *The Five Books of Moses* (New York: Schocken, 1995). See also the list in the previous chapter in the discussion of literary approaches to the Bible.

34. From Fish's influential article "Literature in the Reader: Affective Stylistics," reprinted in *Is There a Text in This Class?* pp. 26–27.

35. Edward L. Greenstein, "An Equivocal Reading of the Sale of Joseph," in Gros Louis, *Literary Interpretations of Biblical Narratives,* 2:116.

36. Ibid., 2:117.

37. See G. Williamson McDiarmid, Deborah Loewenberg Ball, and Charles W. Anderson, "Why Staying One Chapter Ahead Doesn't Really Work: Subject-Specific Pedagogy," in *Knowledge Base for the Beginning Teacher,* ed. M. Reynolds (New York: Pergamon, 1989); and my discussion of this issue in the previous chapter of this volume.

38. Here I distinguish between "commentaries" and readings of literary *theory,* the latter which one does encounter nowadays in universities, though certainly not in the schooling of younger children. Literary theory today is a kind of philosophical endeavor, and I am referring in my text here to specific works of literary interpretation.

39. Robert Scholes, *Textual Power* (New Haven: Yale University Press, 1985), p. 30.

40. This idea is discussed in numerous places in the religious and scholarly literature. See, for one example, the well-known essay by Gershom Scholem "Revela-

tion and Tradition as Religious Categories in Judaism," in his *The Messianic Idea in Judaism and Other Essays on Jewish Spirituality* (New York: Schocken, 1971), pp. 282–304. Or Jacob Neusner, *The Oral Torah* (Atlanta: Scholars Press, 1991).

41. There are ways of looking at the commentaries, studying them in their own right, that also merit exploration.

42. Steven D. Fraade, *From Tradition to Commentary* (Albany: State University of New York Press, 1991), p. 15. See also his interesting notion of a "circulatory view" of rabbinic commentary, on pp. 19–20.

43. For an analysis of Leibowitz's work, see Marla L. Frankel, "A Clarification of Nehama Leibowitz's Approach to the Study and Teaching of Bible" [in Hebrew] (Ph.D. diss., Hebrew University of Jerusalem, 1997). Also: Howard Deitcher, "Between Angels and Mere Mortals: Nehama Leibowitz's Approach to the Study of Biblical Characters," *Journal of Jewish Education* 66, nos. 1–2 (spring/summer 2000): 8–22; and Joy Rochwarger, "Words on Fire: Then and Now—In Memory of Nechama Leibowitz," in *Torah of the Mothers*, ed. Ora Wiskind Elper and Susan Handelman (New York and Jerusalem: Urim, 2000), pp. 57–80.

44. A good example is the scholarly study by Jeremy Cohen, *Be Fertile and Increase, Fill the Earth and Master It: The Ancient and Medieval Career of a Biblical Text* (Ithaca, N.Y.: Cornell University Press, 1989).

45. For example, Nehama Leibowitz, *Studies in Bereshit (Genesis) in the Context of Ancient and Modern Jewish Bible Commentary* (Jerusalem: World Zionist Organization, 1974).

46. Nehama Leibowitz, "Reading a Chapter of *Tanakh*," in *Studies in Jewish Education*, ed. Howard Deitcher and Abraham J. Tannenbaum (Jerusalem: Magnes, 1990), 5:36.

47. James L. Kugel, *The Bible As It Was* (Cambridge, Mass.: Belknap Press of Harvard University Press, 1997), p. 21. Also see my discussion in Holtz, *Back to the Sources*, pp. 177–212.

48. See the excellent discussion of this issue by Robert Alter in "Old Rabbis, New Critics," *The New Republic*, 5 & 12 January 1987, pp. 27–33. Also my "Midrash and Modernity: Can Midrash Serve a Contemporary Religious Discourse?" in *The Uses of Tradition*, ed. Jack Wertheimer (New York: Jewish Theological Seminary, 1992).

49. Sarna, *Understanding Genesis*, p. 214.

50. Leibowitz, *Studies in Bereshit*, p. 407.

51. See my discussion in the previous chapter.

52. Denis Shemilt, "The Devil's Locomotive," *History and Theory* 22, no. 4 (1983): 16.

53. See my discussion of substantive and syntactical structures in the previous chapter.

54. See the comments on this idea in Moshe Halbertal and Tova Hartman Halbertal, "The Yeshiva," in *Philosophers on Education: New Historical Perspectives*, ed. Amélie Oksenberg Rorty (London: Routledge, 1998), pp. 464–65.

55. For a related issue, see Jonathan Cohen's discussion of the problem of defining Jewish philosophy as a discipline in his "Enacting the Eclectic: The Case of Jewish Philosophy," *Journal of Curriculum Studies* 30, no. 2 (1998): 207–31.

56. Fish, *Is There a Text in This Class?* p. 171.

57. Ibid., p. 14.

58. There is a good deal of research currently available on the relationship of a teacher's biography and his or her way of teaching. See, for example: Freema Elbaz, *Teaching Thinking: A Study of Practical Knowledge* (London: Croom Helm, 1983); P. S. Millies, "The Relationship between a Teacher's Life and Teaching," in *Teacher Lore: Learning from Our Experience,* ed. William H. Schubert and William Ayers (White Plains, N.Y.: Longman, 1992); F. Michael Connelly and D. Jean Clandinin, "Personal Practical Knowledge and the Modes of Knowing," in *Learning and Teaching the Ways of Knowing,* ed. Elliot Eisner, *84th Yearbook of the National Society for the Study of Education,* pt. 2 (Chicago: University of Chicago Press, 1985), pp. 174–98; Marilyn Cochran-Smith and Susan L. Lytle, eds., *Inside/Outside: Teacher Research and Knowledge* (New York: Teachers College Press, 1992); and Rosetta Marantz Cohen, *A Lifetime of Teaching: Portraits of Five Veteran High School Teachers* (New York: Teachers College Press, 1991).

59. Through the "apprenticeship of observation" that all teachers experience—by having been students themselves. See Dan Lortie, *Schoolteacher* (Chicago: University of Chicago Press, 1975).

60. Shulman, "Those Who Understand," p. 13.

61. See Miriam Ben-Peretz, *The Teacher-Curriculum Encounter: Freeing Teachers from the Tyranny of Texts* (Albany: State University of New York Press, 1990), on the potential of curriculum and its limitations; and for some of the difficulties, Sharon Feiman-Nemser and Deborah Loewenberg Ball, "Using Textbooks and Teachers' Guides: A Dilemma for Beginning Teachers and Teacher Educators," *Curriculum Inquiry* 18 (1988): 401–23.

62. Deborah Loewenberg Ball and David K. Cohen, "Reform by the Book: What Is—or Might Be—the Role of Curriculum Materials in Teacher Learning and Instructional Reform?" *Educational Researcher* 25, no. 9 (1996): 6.

63. Seymour Rossel, *A Child's Bible* (West Orange, N.J.: Behrman House, 1988), p. 7.

64. Ibid.

65. Ibid., p. 43.

66. Ibid., p. 118.

67. Ibid.

68. Alter, *The Art of Biblical Narrative,* p. 12.

69. Thus, in the Tower of Babel story, we read, "God saw the bricks becoming a city and a tower. God watched as the hearts of the people became as hard as bricks. The people of the earth stopped loving one another. They forgot how to love God," etc. (Rossel, *A Child's Bible,* p. 41). See the original version in Gen.

11:5–7, by contrast, where none of these motivational details is given. In answer to those who would argue that *A Child's Bible* adds these details because it is meant for *children,* see the retelling in Shirley Newman, *A Child's Introduction to Torah* (New York: Behrman House and Melton Research Center, 1972), for an approach much more faithful to the original.

70. See, by contrast, Sarna's views on the importance of the "intellectual challenge" involved in studying the Bible, *Understanding Genesis,* pp. xxii–xxiii.

71. Miriam Lorber and Judith Shamir, *Gateway to Torah* (New York: Ktav, 1991).

72. Rosenberg, "Biblical Narrative," pp. 62–63.

73. Note Buber's influence on a more recent book, Gabriel Josipovici's *The Book of God: A Response to the Bible* (New Haven: Yale University Press, 1988), in which the author says that we should look at the Bible not "as a book to be deciphered, or a story to be told," but rather, "we should think of it as a person. We do not decipher people, we encounter them" (p. 307).

74. In Martin Buber, *On the Bible: Eighteen Studies,* ed. Nahum N. Glatzer (New York: Schocken, 1968), p. 4.

75. Ibid.

76. Ibid., p. 5.

77. Norman Cohen, *Self, Struggle and Change* (Woodstock, Vt.: Jewish Lights, 1997), p. 13.

78. Ibid., pp. 14–15.

79. Ibid.

80. For political readings, one might turn to Arthur Waskow's *Godwrestling* (New York: Schocken, 1978); or Judith Plaskow's feminist readings in *Standing Again at Sinai* (New York: Harper and Row, 1990). For a more "spiritual" approach, one could turn to Lawrence Kushner's *God Was in This Place and I, I Did Not Know* (Woodstock, Vt.: Jewish Lights, 1993).

81. Leonard Gardner, *Genesis: The Teacher's Guide* (New York: Melton Research Center, 1966).

82. See the discussion of the early years of the Melton Bible curriculum in Ruth Zielenziger, "A History of the Bible Program of the Melton Research Center with Special Reference to the Curricular Principles on Which It Is Based" (Ph.D. diss., Jewish Theological Seminary, 1989).

83. Ruth Zielenziger, *Genesis: A New Teacher's Guide* (New York: Melton Research Center, 1979).

84. Gardner, *Genesis,* p. 210.

85. Ibid., p. 211.

86. I've taken both examples from Sarna's *Understanding Genesis,* the original basis of the curriculum, which, despite its emphasis on a contextual framework and comparisons with the ancient Near Eastern sources, still asserts these basic ideas and values. The first example is found on p. 18, the second on p. 28. Looking at Gardner or Zielenziger, *Genesis: A New Teacher's Guide,* makes the case even more clearly.

87. There is, however, an interesting convergence between the Melton approach and that advocated by Zvi Adar, an influential Israeli educator of the same period. See Adar's *Humanistic Values in the Bible* (New York: Reconstructionist, 1967), and his article "The Teaching of the Bible in Israel and the Problem of Religious Education," Scripta Hierosolymitana 13 (Jerusalem: Magnes, 1963). See Zielenziger, "A History of the Bible Program," pp. 33–35.

88. Burton Cohen and Joseph Schwab, "Practical Logic: Problems of Ethical Decision." The article originally appeared in *The American Behavioral Scientist* 8, no. 8 (April 1965) and was subsequently reprinted as an appendix to Gardner's *Teacher's Guide*. The page numbers in the references below refer to the reprint in Gardner.

89. Ibid., p. 493.

90. Ibid.

91. Ibid., p. 494. Also see Burton Cohen, "The Teaching of Deliberation in the Jewish School," in *Studies in Jewish Education,* ed. Michael Rosenak (Jerusalem: Magnes, 1984), 2:122–35. For an interesting perspective on this type of approach to moral decision making, see Michael Oakeshott's "The Tower of Babel," in *Rationalism in Politics and Other Essays* (London: Methuen, 1962), pp. 59–79.

92. Cohen, "The Teaching of Deliberation," p. 494.

93. Ibid.

94. See, for example, Eliot Dorff, "Study Leads to Action," *Religious Education* 75, no. 2 (March/April 1980): 171–92.

95. See the excellent discussion of these issues in Norman Lamm, *Torah Lishmah: Torah for Torah's Sake in the Works of Rabbi Hayyim of Volozhin and His Contemporaries* (Hoboken, N.J.: Ktav, 1989). For the educational implications of the question, see the sophisticated analysis by Michael Rosenak, *Roads to the Palace: Jewish Texts and Teaching* (Providence: Berghahn, 1995), esp. pp. 231–34; see also my discussion in Holtz, *Finding Our Way,* pp. 212–30.

96. See the discussion in Isadore Twersky, *Introduction to the Code of Maimonides (Mishneh Torah)* (New Haven: Yale University Press, 1980), pp. 244–54.

97. This was an important element in the thinking of David Ben-Gurion, the first prime minister of Israel. See the discussion by Anita Shapira, "Ben-Gurion and the Bible" [in Hebrew], in her *New Jews, Old Jews* (Tel Aviv: Am Oved, 1997), pp. 217–47. For some of the complications inherent in this approach, see Nadav Ne'eman, "Taking the Bible Out of the Jewish Bookshelf" [in Hebrew], *Ha'aretz,* 2 July 1998, p. B-13.

98. See Zielenziger, "A History of the Bible Program," pp. 38–43.

CHAPTER FOUR

From Orientations to Goals:
What Should the Teacher Do?

Practical Guidance for the Teacher

In what way can a knowledge of orientations offer help for teachers? The map of Bible orientations outlined in the previous chapter should serve a practical purpose. It should help teachers or teacher educators improve their work. Let us consider a number of practical implications that flow out of this exploration.

First, understanding orientations allows teachers to locate their approaches to subject matter in reliable, scholarly sources or in well-established educational points of view. It is certainly true, as I pointed out in the previous chapter, that not every orientation is rooted in academic scholarship, but those that are not based in the world of university research—such as Nehama Leibowitz's approach—carry a different kind of pedagogic authority that also allows them to help a teacher gain a sense of perspective and direction.

Second, the notion of multiple orientations (consider the three readings of English literary texts at the beginning of chapter 3) emanates out of a view that no single reading can encompass the entirety of any great text. Edward Greenstein makes this point in discussing ways of interpreting the Bible:

> I take the position that different theoretical approaches to literature serve the useful function of generating diverse strategies by which to read and interpret texts. Rather than choose to delimit meaning by adhering to one particular school or method of criticism, readers may elect to adopt and adapt reading approaches from a variety of theories. . . .

> No theory can stand up to all critical challenge and monopolize the way we read. . . . The meaning of a text is not self-evident but is made by readers, and the same reader may find a number of different reading strategies both valid and enriching by making meaning on many levels alternatively.[1]

Indirectly, Greenstein suggests guidance for teachers. Expressed in the language that we have been using, he might argue that a good classroom requires a variety of orientations because the hidden message of such teaching for students is the validation of "making meaning on many levels alternatively."

Third, Greenstein's point of view, coming out of the scholarly world, parallels suggestions made by educators in their call for teachers to develop "flexible subject-matter understanding," a term introduced in the previous chapter. That kind of flexibility allows teachers to respond to different kinds of questions and issues that learners may have. Not every learner will resonate with every orientation. Some students—both children and adults—will revel in the close reading of text that we see in New Critical approaches to reading Bible. Others will find that orientation frustrating. Those students may respond better to the moralistic-didactic orientation because it gives them a clear sense of answers to questions that concern them. Others may find the contextual approach much more compelling.

Flexible subject-matter knowledge means that teachers have the ability to make connections across topics and disciplines and are able to make use of the contributions of scholarship and their potential for education. Having a perspective on orientations gives teachers a bird's-eye view of the subject matter that leads to flexible knowledge.

Fourth, a knowledge of orientations allows teachers to match the text they are teaching to the appropriate orientation and pedagogy. In other words, understanding orientations pushes a teacher to consider questions such as, What is the relationship between any specific text and the orientation that might be employed to teach it? Does the text determine the orientation, or is any orientation possible with any text?

It seems fairly clear that some texts "call out" for certain specific orientations while others are more open-ended. To return to our literary examples from chapter 3, for instance, it is possible to imagine a very different class about *The Merchant of Venice*. In this class, the teacher would eschew the historically oriented lesson described in chapter 3 and conduct the class in the spirit of New Criticism, analyzing word patterns and imagery throughout the play. Or one could imagine Stanley Fish using a reader-response orientation to teach the same play, as he did in his famous study of Milton's *Paradise Lost*, an early landmark in reader-response criticism.[2]

Yet it would be hard to picture a teacher using a historical/contextual orientation to teach "The edge" by Richard Jones. Similarly, there are biblical texts that call out for various literary approaches, whether they be New Critical or reader-response; teaching other texts (say, texts on sacrificial practices in Leviticus) with such orientations might seem peculiar indeed.

Finally, understanding orientations allows teachers to clarify their goals and pedagogy. When I locate my teaching within a particular orientation, I am at the same time exploring the goals that I have in teaching the text before me. Am I a teacher who views the Bible as a source of personal wisdom? If that is my orientation, then my goals in teaching any particular text will try to get students to that understanding. Am I a teacher who views the Bible as a way of understanding our people's past? Once again, the way I view the classroom and its outcomes will be influenced by that orientation.

In addition, it's worth asking if my orientation determines my pedagogic strategies, or is any strategy possible with any text? Once again, certain kinds of strategies seem to go particularly well with certain orientations, though one can imagine many different kinds of teaching approaches with virtually any orientation. Classroom discussion, for example, seems to fit well with literary analysis, yet one can equally see teachers using frontal lectures to implement the same kind of orientation. The moralistic-didactic approach may, on the surface, look to be an orientation that cries out for frontal presentation, but talented teachers could create lessons based around group work to accomplish the same ends. In general, it appears that certain orientations "lean" toward particular modes of classroom organization or teaching approaches, but the map may be more flexible in this regard than it seems at first. The practical uses of orientations are summarized in the chart found on the next page.

How Might a Knowledge of Orientations Help Teachers?

Such knowledge can help teachers . . .

1. Locate their approaches to subject matter in reliable, scholarly sources

2. Support a diversity of readings and interpretations of texts—there is no one right reading

3. Develop "flexible subject-matter understanding"—
   - To respond to different kinds of questions and issues that learners may have
   - To make connections across topics and disciplines
   - To make use of contributions of scholarship and their potential for education

4. Match the text they are teaching to the appropriate orientation/ pedagogy

5. Clarify goals and pedagogy

Is There a "Best" Orientation?

I have not, however, addressed what may be the largest question raised by our map. Namely, is one orientation preferable—that is, is there a "best way" to teach the Bible? Of course, by its very nature such a question is virtually impossible to answer. The question of "best" needs to be preceded by asking a number of other questions: What is the age of the student? What is the educational environment? What are the stated goals of the educational institution? If, in other words, this is a class for adults with little Jewish learning, I may choose one orientation, while if it is a class for children in a school that sees its main goal as developing committed, practicing Jews, I might have another.

But if I am pressed to give an answer—if the reader of this book were to ask, So what would *you* do in teaching the Bible?—let me try to offer some suggestions.

First, I have to say that all the orientations in the map are attractive to me! That is, I don't believe that any one orientation is *a priori* better than any other. I do believe, however, that certain orientations are less likely to work in certain educational environments than others. Here the question of milieu enters the picture once again. The orientations on the map might be superimposed on an image of the various contemporary Jewish denominations. Not every orientation is going to be acceptable for every Jewish point of view. And even where certain orientations are "acceptable," they may not be terribly welcomed. Orthodox institutions tend to focus on the *parshanut* orientation, while Reform institutions are drawn to the contextual orientation and a version of "The Bible Leads to Action" (in that case, the prophetic tradition of the Bible and the social action message of Reform Judaism). Orthodox and Conservative environments tend to read "The Bible Leads to Action" as a focus on the obligations of the mitzvot (though Orthodox and Conservative differ in emphasis and approach). Conservative schools have focused a good deal on the ideational orientation and the literary criticism orientation. None of these is set in stone, but it is rare to see the contextual orientation in an Orthodox school or the *parshanut* orientation in a Reform institution. The ideologies of the movements, therefore, have an impact on the orientations that one would find in their educational institutions.

Moreover, some orientations are more appropriate to certain ages than others. That is, I think that the moralistic-didactic orientation is not terribly appropriate to adults but that the ideational orientation is. This is simply a reflection on the nature of adult development and the needs that adult learners express in attending Jewish adult education classes.

Because of the developmental issues involved, it seems to me that the map of orientations presents a kind of *curricular* resource. How could any individual teacher or educational institution take the bird's-eye view of the subject matter that knowing orientations provides and use it as a planning guide for a curriculum? In order to do so, we would ask questions like: What orientations would children in the early years in the school come to experience? How would they be prepared to gain the skills that would allow them to study using certain orientations later on in the school or in adulthood? Thus, one could see the decoding-comprehension orientation as a constant throughout the school, beginning at an early age and aimed at giving students the skills they would need for other orientations. One might view it as a kind of foundational orientation. I personally am not drawn to the moralistic-didactic orientation, but I recognize that young children can sometimes benefit from the sense of surety that such an orientation gives them: it helps them feel that the Bible really does speak to them and offers guidance about life.

The literary criticism orientation (personally, it is much closer to my own inclinations) would come into play around the sixth or seventh grade, but even younger students will be learning the skills of close reading that prepare them for *explication de texte* later on. The *parshanut* orientation would be introduced at around the same time as the literary criticism orientation or perhaps slightly later.

There are no hard-and-fast rules about these developmental issues. Experience and the findings of developmental psychology help us make certain decisions. Other orientations may be possible at any age. I don't think, for example, that personalization is limited by one's developmental stage.

The curricular perspective laid out above is one piece of advice that I would offer, but if I were to make specific suggestions for the individual classroom, I would emphasize the importance of presenting *an eclectic of appropriate orientations*. "Appropriate" in that phrase is meant to account for the developmental issues. That is, once we recognize that certain orientations are best suited to certain ages, we are still left with a number of possible choices. To my mind, presenting students with a variety of orientations makes a good deal of sense. I have presented many of the reasons earlier in this chapter: such an approach validates many different readings of texts; it responds to different kinds of learners and their different questions and concerns; and it allows for the adaptation of pedagogy to the specific qualities of particular biblical texts.

In her study of novice and expert Bible teachers, for example, Gail Dorph describes an experienced Bible teacher teaching a lesson on the Tower of Babel story.[3] She pushes the students to pay close attention to the specific words in the biblical narrative; she asks them to consider motivations of characters; she tells them about ziggurats, the towers that Mesopotamians built as temples; and she relates a rabbinic midrash about the origin of different languages. Thus, we see in this example a teacher who manages to weave in contextual and literary criticism orientations along with examples from *parshanut*. As Dorph points out:

> By creating a lesson in which multiple solutions to the questions raised by the Torah text are generated and no single solution is selected or preferred, she teaches her students that the study of the Torah is an open-ended inquiry.[4]

There is no reason that an eclectic of orientations needs to be found in every single lesson. It is perfectly legitimate, in my view, to have a lesson that focuses on the historical background of a particular biblical text and does very little in the way of the Jewish interpretive tradition. But over the course of time, students should be presented with a wide range of views and pedagogic approaches. Keeping one's eye on the map of orientations helps attain that goal.

What about Our Larger Goals?

Although an orientation touches upon a teacher's purposes, in general it is uncommon to see a teacher's orientation that flows out of a well-worked-out philosophical position or a profound engagement with the subject matter being taught. As practitioners, teachers tend to be motivated by an intuition of "what works" in the classroom, and the definition of "working" is related to the way that students seem to be engaged with the material, or at least not "causing trouble."[5] The map of orientations should be viewed, therefore, not as a theoretical construct of pedagogical approaches based on philosophical positions, but rather as a kind of "middle range" representation of current Bible teaching approaches. Obviously, even this particular map is not exhaustive, but it does cover some of the most commonly found examples of the way teachers think about—and practice—contemporary Bible pedagogy.

Though the orientations are not examples of what might be called "philosophy in action," in *indirect* ways such orientations touch upon a larger sense of goals and principles.[6] They are connected to philosophy but are focused upon practice, on what we *do* when we teach Bible more than *why* we do what we do.[7]

The teacher who uses the *parshanut* orientation, for instance, may have a larger goal in mind. That goal may be very well defined; it may be rooted in a larger, philosophical justification, but more often than not, it may simply be a version of "that's the way we teach Bible around here" or "that's the way I was taught Bible when I was a student." Israel Scheffler, writing about the notion of "justifications" for curricular decisions, has commented on this phenomenon:

> When we decide broad educational issues, we are often asking not merely what jibes with American practice, past or present, but what is generally justified, whether or not it is sanctioned by practice. The desire to evade this general question is understandable because it is difficult. But this evasion, I think, is responsible for much of the inadequacy of value-discussions in education.[8]

What needs to be added, then, to the notion of orientations is a more abstract discussion of purposes: What kinds of justifications could be suggested for approaches to teaching Bible? What concepts, indeed, may cut across a variety of orientations? Hence, we might think about orientations as the signpost of one's goals in approaching any particular biblical text. But standing behind any orientation is a larger goal—a sense of one's ultimate purpose in teaching this entire subject matter.

I want to turn now to explore such larger purposes, "justifications" for the teaching of Bible. I am going to focus on one specific overarching goal that is particularly powerful for me—the notion of "Bible as truth." I want to explore the implications of that answer to the question, Why teach the Bible? But before I get to that idea, I want to touch upon two other conceptions that answer the same question. These do not necessarily contradict my primary focus but will serve as a backdrop to our more extended inquiry.

The Bible Is Interesting

One educational justification for teaching the Bible cuts across a number of our orientations, namely, the Bible is an *interesting* text. The quality of being interesting as an educational justification may seem self-evident, but many subject areas are plagued by students' perceptions that the area at hand is not sufficiently compelling. Of course, in education, the question of the inherent "interestingness" of any subject matter is confounded with the almost impossible dilemma of disentangling a student's perception of the content learned from that student's experience of how the material was taught. In other words, is the subject boring, or does the subject appear to be boring because it was taught in a boring way? Teaching and learning are inextricably bound up with each other. The subject matter is interesting only insofar as students perceive it to be of interest. Hence, Eleanor Duckworth's reminder that good teaching is about providing students with opportunities for "the having of wonderful ideas."[9]

But setting aside this problem for now, it is clear that the Bible is inherently interesting (or potentially interesting) in a number of different ways. First, it is a varied and intellectually challenging work, and the excitement of reading the Bible produces its own psychic rewards. R. S. Peters points out that "absence of boredom"[10] is an enduring justification of education throughout human history. "Arguments for education in terms of absorption and satisfaction,"[11] as he puts it, have an old and honorable lineage.

Beyond absence of boredom, of course, studying the Bible is a demanding intellectual activity. It is that very fact, Israel Scheffler shows, that leads to the powerful emotional dimension of such pursuits. For Scheffler, the "cognitive" and "affective" are inseparable.[12] Thus, Scheffler speaks about emotions that can occur during a scientific inquiry—such as "the joy of verification" and "the feeling of surprise"—arguing that intellectually challenging experiences can be emotionally rewarding. The demanding work of studying the Bible offers these same powerful emotional rewards, too: the student is involved in the pleasure of learning a difficult thing. Joseph Schwab's memorable description of the "eros" of educational endeavors is particularly apt:

> Not only the means, however, but also the ends of liberal education involve the Eros. For the end includes not only knowledge gained but knowledge desired and knowledge sought. The outcome of a successful liberal curriculum is *actively* intelligent people. They *like* good pictures, good books, good music, good movies. They *find pleasure* in planning their active lives and carrying out the planned action. They hanker to make, to create, whether the object is knowledge mastered, art appreciated or actions patterned and directed. In short, a curriculum is not complete which does not move the Eros, as well as the mind of the young, from where it is to where it might better be.[13]

The Bible is interesting in other ways as well. Studying the Bible allows people to enter into the world of the past; more than that, into the world of *their own people's* past. In that sense, we might say, the study of the Bible is the study of one's family tree.

This dimension of tracing the past fits well with the orientation I have called the "contextual approach." Within that orientation, the emphasis is on discovering the historically rich world out of which the Bible emerged. It entails entering the life of the ancient Near East, with its strangeness, beauty, and complexities. But the justification that sees the Bible as interesting also plays a significant role in orientations beyond the contextual approach. After all, the interestingness of the subject matter—provided, as noted above, that the pedagogy is engaging—is not limited to historical contextual approaches to the text. Literary studies and *parshanut,* for example, are both, at least in potential, exercises of great intellectual interest.

The Bible Is Our Obligation

The justification from the point of view of "interest" is essentially a "hedonistic"[14] argument. We study because it is pleasurable to do so. Wanting to inculcate in students the pleasure of learning is a powerful and admirable goal.

But throughout Jewish history, the study of Bible has always had a different kind of justification as well: the study of Torah as a religious obligation. Study is a commandment that observant Jews must fulfill and is therefore deeply embedded in the cultural norms of the community. Moreover, that obligation is closely linked to another traditional concept—*Torah lishmah,* the study of Torah "for its own sake."

Torah lishmah is a complex notion much discussed within the Jewish tradition. What does it mean for an activity to be "for its own sake"? Is this meant to be an example of a completely "noninstrumental" activity—the only reward is doing the activity itself? Or do other, less obvious, benefits come into play—honor in the community, rewards in the cosmic realm? Is *Torah lishmah* a Jewish version of "art for art's sake," or does the phrase have a very different valence? Even the talmudic statement that one should not seek public acclaim for one's learning but "learn out of love, and honor will come in the end" suggests that, in the long run, one will not toil anonymously—after all, honor will come![15]

But whether the student of *Torah lishmah* does so out of "pure" motives (if such are possible at all) or not, this mode of learning surely fits R. S. Peters's useful concept of "worth-while activities." Peters asks the question at the heart of any curricular inquiry: Why do this rather than that? What are the possible justifications in making the choices that are unavoidable in the give-and-take of making curricular decisions? Peters reviews a number of different ways of answering his question, among other things considering the ways that playing games might be considered a "worth-while" activity as much as learning about science, mathematics, or literature. Is studying Torah also a kind of game playing? Peters, I believe, would answer no, for the same reason that he views the study of the classic academic disciplines significantly different from playing even "serious" games like chess.

Why? Because playing games, as interesting as that may be, as "pure"—as "for its own sake"—as it may be, misses the essential element of learning that we experience when studying science, history, or the Bible:

> Science, history, literary appreciation, philosophy, and other such cultural activities . . . can be, and to a large extent are, pursued for the sake of values intrinsic to them rather than for the sake of extrinsic ends. But their cognitive concerns and far-ranging cognitive content give them a value denied to other more circumscribed activities which leads us to call them serious pursuits. They are "serious" and cannot be considered merely as if they were particularly delectable pastimes, because they consist largely in the explanation, assessment, and illumination of the different facets of life. They thus insensibly change a man's view of the world. . . . A man who devotes himself to a game . . . does not thereby equip himself with a cognitive content that spills over and transforms his view of other things in life. . . .

> The point, then, about activities such as science, philosophy and history is that although they are like games in that they are disinterested activities which can be pursued at set times and places, . . . a person who has pursued them systematically develops conceptual schemes and forms of appraisal which transform everything else that he does.[16]

Biblical study, then, is obviously a "worth-while" activity because it has the potential to imbue the student with "a cognitive content that spills over and transforms his view of other things in life."

The Bible as Truth

To say that studying the Bible is, like other great academic pursuits, potentially transformative of the student's life, is to suggest that it inhabits a particular and very special universe, a place where the primary concern is nothing less than the pursuit of truth. As Peters puts it:

> Being concerned about truth has another type of worth. It can be regarded as having a worth which is independent of its benefit. Indeed, the state of mind of one who is determined to find out what is true . . . can be regarded as an ultimate value which provides one of the criteria of benefit. . . . Someone who values truth in this way may find the constant effort to free his mind from prejudice and error painful; he may sometimes find it wearisome and boring; but it matters to him supremely, even if he falls short of the ideal which he accepts.[17]

What does it mean to concerned with "truth"? I will now turn to various approaches to this knotty issue.

To begin, I will consider the ideas of the contemporary philosopher Hans-Georg Gadamer.[18] For Gadamer, the essential goal in confronting a text (or any work of art) from the past is to experience its *truth*. In this regard, Gadamer pushes us to listen carefully, respectfully, to works of the past, to take those texts seriously without rushing to judgment. As one scholar has claimed, for Gadamer, "the first principle of a hermeneutical interpretation of a text is to come to an agreement about the truth of the subject matter in question. But to come to an agreement or understanding, one has to recognize the integrity and independence of the viewpoint of the other."[19] That is, we need to take the truth claims of the text very seriously indeed.[20]

Gadamer views much of modern hermeneutics as an attempt to run away from the question of the truth of the text and to replace it instead with a concern for clarifying the historical or personal circumstances under which the text was composed. Gadamer attributes this move to the German philosopher Friedrich Schleiermacher (1768–1834) and his attempt to do what Gadamer views as essentially an impossible task: to "reveal the true meaning of a work of art and guard against misunderstanding and anachronistic interpretation" by reproducing "the writer's original process of production" and the historical context in which he or she lived.[21] Instead of truth, the interpreter in the Schleiermacher mode is interested in "reconstruct[ing] the original intentions of writers . . . and the circumstances of their lives."[22] Especially in a world in which claims of truth are suspect to begin with, the "romantic" hermeneutics of Schleiermacher, Wilhelm Dilthey (1833–1911), and others—with their focus on the historical, contextual dimension of interpretation—came to play an increasingly significant role in intellectual life. But Gadamer believes that the resort to exploring historical context and writers' motivations is an inadequate response to the texts of the past:

> Hermeneutic work is based on a polarity of familiarity and strangeness; but this polarity is not to be regarded psychologically, with Schleiermacher, as the range that covers the mystery of individuality, but truly hermeneutically—i.e., in regard to what has been said: the language in which the text addresses us, the story that it tells us. Here too there is a tension. It is in the play between the traditionary text's strangeness and familiarity to us, between being a historically intended, distanciated object and belonging to a tradition. *The true locus of hermeneutics is this in-between.*[23]

The tension between the familiar and the strange abides at the heart of Gadamer's interpretive view. In essence, the Schleiermacher approach collapses the familiar-strange polarity into a merely psychological focus (specifically on the artist) or a contextual focus (on the world in which the text has been created). And, according to Gadamer, this destroys the crucial tension involved in taking any traditional text seriously. The problem Gadamer describes here parallels quite closely the approach of biblical studies, at least in the world of the university, during the past century. Gadamer would, I believe, criticize biblical studies in which scholars tried to "explain" the Bible by putting their energies into describing the historical, linguistic, and cultural context in which the Bible was produced. These scholars, Gadamer might charge, mistakenly believe that they should read the Bible in the hermeneutical manner of Schleiermacher. By not seriously confronting the potential "truth" of the text, Gadamer believes that we have abandoned the most important dimension of interpretive work, "to understand the content of what is said, and only secondarily to isolate and understand another's meaning as such."[24]

In what way can a text like the Bible teach truth? A number of contemporary thinkers have grappled with this question in thinking about the ways that the study of literature may have an impact on the lives of students—beyond the level of intellectual engagement (what I have called above "the Bible is interesting"). These views have important implications for the study of Bible, though, as I will try to show below, and there are also significant differences because of the particular nature of biblical study.

One approach to this question has been articulated by the philosopher of education Harvey Siegel. Siegel wants to ask "[H]ow can fiction teach? What are the pedagogical possibilities of fiction? What sorts of lessons can be taught?"[25] He argues that novels "can add to our understanding of philosophical issues by making clear to us the motivations and felt reasons undergirding alternative views. A very fine novelist can make such reasons come alive and drive home sorts of reasons not open to more conventional modes of teaching."[26]

In *The Brothers Karamazov,* for example, Dostoyevsky deals with a number of powerful philosophical issues—the problem of evil, the meaning of suffering, and the conflict of belief and unbelief, among others. "Felt reasons," a phrase that Siegel uses as a kind of technical term, have a "visceral quality" that allows us to "feel the force of reasons . . . in entirely different ways than we feel the force of the . . . same reasons in other circumstances."[27] It is not that Dostoyevsky offers philosophical ideas that are "particularly original or forceful, if taken out the context of the novel."[28] Rather, the living embodied context of fiction changes our experience of the reasons offered. The living, breathing characters of a novel, enmeshed in circumstances that are, if not familiar, extremely real to us, make reading a novel by Dostoyevsky about the nature of evil palpably different from reading a work like Hume's *Dialogues Concerning Natural Religion,* even though both may deal with some of the same issues. The felt reasons presented in fiction are not different "from ordinary propositional reasons. [They are] ordinary reasons whose power to move people is made obvious or manifest by the way in which those reasons . . . are portrayed. Felt reasons are not a different kind of reason; they are rather a particular *kind* of *presentation* of reasons."[29]

Reading literary works of this sort is crucial to the practice of (and here, Siegel uses Scheffler's term) "the rationality theory of teaching, which places the offering and exchange of reasons at the center of teaching activities."[30] Examples from fiction represent points of view in intense and living ways, making them come alive for the reader or learner.

The embodiment of philosophical disputation in fiction allows us to view reading and teaching literature as a kind of moral enterprise—it is meant to have an effect on the reader that is not "merely" aesthetic. We can follow that line of argument into other realms as well. The reading and teaching of great literature can, in the view of some, actually make us better, more ethical human beings.

Richard Rorty, for example, argues that certain books can "help us become less cruel."[31] He divides these books into two types: books like *Uncle Tom's Cabin*, which "help us see how social practices which we have taken for granted have made us cruel"; and books "about the ways in which particular types of people are cruel to other particular sorts of people."[32] These latter books might include George Eliot's *Middlemarch* or Dickens's *Bleak House*. When we read these books, we begin to realize the ways that "our private obsessions with the achievement of a certain sort of perfection may make us oblivious to the pain and humiliation we are causing" others.[33] Rorty's definition of the power of books to affect the way we think about others, the way we might avoid causing cruelty, might influence a pedagogic stance toward the teaching of a biblical text like the story of Jacob and Esau. When Esau realizes that Jacob has tricked him out of Isaac's blessing, we read one of the most poignant scenes in the entire Bible, " 'Have you but one blessing, Father? Bless me, too, Father!' And Esau wept aloud" (Gen. 27:38). Teaching such a text, Rorty might argue, has the potential to move the student away from cruelty.

Siegel and Rorty move in the direction of the role of literature as a tool in the reader's ethical development. This position has most powerfully been articulated in the work of two other thinkers, Martha Nussbaum and Wayne C. Booth. In Nussbaum's collection of essays, *Love's Knowledge,* she states her desire to look at works of literature as "indispensable to a philosophical inquiry in the ethical sphere: not by any means sufficient, but sources of insight without which inquiry cannot be complete."[34] Such a view, according to Nussbaum, swims against the tide of most literary criticism, writing that assumes "that any work that attempts to ask of a literary text questions about how we might live, treating the work as addressed to the reader's practical interests and needs, and as being in some sense about our lives, must be hopelessly naïve, reactionary, and insensitive to the complexities of literary form and intertextual referentiality."

Such "ethical criticism" need not lead to overly simplistic, moralistic tracts, she argues. Rather, "far from insisting that all literature must play some single, simple role in human life, the best ethical criticism, ancient and modern, has insisted on the complexity and variety revealed to us in literature, appealing to that complexity to cast doubt on reductive theories."[35]

Love's Knowledge tries to demonstrate such an approach with essays on a variety of literary works, including novels by Henry James and Dickens. This is a rich and complex work, impossible to summarize in a few pages, but the main point that is of relevance to us is Nussbaum's belief that we can find in fiction ways of thinking about the fundamental question of how one should live. Fiction does this in a number of ways, but one of the most salient is that it shows us "the ethical crudeness of moralities based exclusively on general rules, and to demand for ethics a much finer responsiveness to the concrete."[36] In another book, *Poetic Justice,* she seeks to spell out the way that literature "has the potential to make a distinctive contribution to our public life."[37] How? By giving us the ability "to imagine what it is like to live the life of another person who might, given changes in circumstance, be oneself or one of one's loved ones."[38]

It is obvious that Nussbaum leans toward fiction of a particular sort—the "realist" novels of Dickens, George Eliot, and James represent well her interest in the "concrete" and the "ordinary."[39] There is far less interest in Joyce in her writing, for example. But Nussbaum provides a particularly appropriate lens to look at the goals of teaching Bible. This is not because the Bible is precisely like a nineteenth-century realist novel, of course. Obviously, one major difference is that the Bible consists of many genres, not just a realist narrative one. Along with familiar narratives, we find law, prophecy, wisdom literature (e.g., Proverbs), and poetry. But for educators, the narrative portions of the Bible are those most often taught, and here the power of "ethical criticism" is relevant indeed.

The gap between the Bible and modern fiction is not only to be found in the realm of genre. There are vast differences between, say, the

Joseph story and James's *Princess Casamassima*. The fine details of place and nuanced readings of internal states that one finds in Henry James are not present in the Bible, nor will we find the careful descriptions of a character's appearance or the assured voice of an omniscient narrator such as we might encounter in a novel by Dickens or George Eliot. The way the Bible tells its stories is markedly different from the way that later fiction, like the novel, tells its stories.[40]

But despite these discontinuities between the novel and the Bible, we see congruities of great significance that make the comparisons between these two literatures very instructive for our pedagogical project. In the Bible, we see people struggling with questions of right and wrong, death and life, good and evil, all in muted tones of gray, similar to the complexities of presentation found in the fiction that Booth and Nussbaum examine. In what way was Joseph to blame for the troubles he encountered with his brothers? How was his father, Jacob, culpable as well? What did it mean to be the favored son? In what way was the special coat both a symbol and a burden? Looking at Edward Greenstein's article "An Equivocal Reading of the Sale of Joseph,"[41] for example, we see an embodiment of Nussbaum's words about "the worth and richness of plural qualitative thinking."[42] If we look at the David and Bathsheva story (particularly as read by Meir Sternberg),[43] we see exemplification of Nussbaum's words about how the "choice between two qualitatively different actions or commitments, when on account of circumstances one cannot pursue both, is or can be tragic."[44]

We dwell on narrative not only because some of the most enduring and memorable elements of the Bible are its narratives but also because narrative itself has such a deep hold on the human species. We *live* through narratives; they define us as individuals and as parts of a larger society. Thus, reading and teaching biblical narratives help us and our students make sense of their lives as human beings, as part of a culture. "Why is it," asks Mark Johnson, "that we turn to literary texts for our moral education? Why do we learn more from narratives than from academic moral philosophy about what it is to be human, about the contingencies of life, about the kinds of lives we most want to lead and about what is involved in trying to lead such lives?"[45]

"The key to the answer," he says, "is that *our lives ultimately have a narrative structure* [emphasis added]. It is in sustained narrative, therefore, that we come closest to observing and participating in the reality of life as it is actually experienced and lived." Placing narrative at the heart of the curriculum of biblical studies, then, is no whim, no attempt to dodge the difficulties of other biblical genres (and, as we shall see in the next chapter, there are difficulties aplenty in biblical narrative!). It might, in fact, be our first obligation to those whom we teach, no matter what age they may be. As Alasdair MacIntyre memorably put it:

> [M]an is in his actions and practice, as well as in his fictions, essentially a story-telling animal. He is not essentially, but becomes through his history, a teller of stories that aspire to truth. But the key question for men is not about their own authorship; I can only answer the question "What am I to do?" if I can answer the prior question "Of what story or stories do I find myself a part?" We enter human society, that is, with one or more imputed characters . . . and we have to learn what they are in order to be able to understand how others respond to us and how our responses to them are apt to be construed. It is through hearing stories about wicked stepmothers, lost children, good but misguided kings, wolves that suckled twin boys . . . that children learn or mislearn both what a child and what a parent is, what the cast of characters may be in the drama into which they have been born and what the ways of the world are. Deprive children of stories and you leave them unscripted, anxious stutterers in their actions as in their words. Hence there is no way to give us an understanding of any society, including our own, except through the stock of stories which constitute its initial dramatic resources.[46]

Of all the writers exploring "ethical criticism," there is arguably none as influential as the literary critic Wayne C. Booth. Particularly in his profound and monumental volume *The Company We Keep: An Ethics of Fiction,* Booth has explored the complexities of encountering books for the ways in which they can affect the reader's life.[47] This lengthy and far-ranging work is impossible to summarize in our context here, but I want to focus on one aspect of Booth's thinking, namely, the way that learning has an impact on one's ethical sensibility. Or, as Nussbaum puts it, "what becomes of readers *as* they read?"[48]

Booth invents a term, "coduction," to refer to the kinds of conversations that we need to have in which "we arrive at our sense of value in narrative."[49] Whenever I read a text, I am constantly viewing it against the "backdrop of my long personal history of untraceably complex experiences of other stories and persons."[50] More than that, I am engaged in a community of like-minded readers, also trying to puzzle out the moral implications of that which I have read. As we talk to one another, the work is "transformed by us as we hold our conversations about it."[51] What Booth is speaking about, with his strong emphasis on the power of conversation, is a model of teaching. This is not, it should be clear, the "moralistic-didactic orientation" that I wrote about in chapter 3. There are no easy answers to the questions of "truth" here, no moral prescriptions. Instead, there is a generating of moral vision and self-reflection within the classroom discourse. Booth's analysis of hermeneutical principles is, it turns out to be, an argument for a kind of pedagogy.

I have spoken here about the "Bible as truth" in terms of the text's ethical power, in the way that Nussbaum and Booth have adumbrated the concept. But it is appropriate to add another dimension of "truth" as well. The Bible may speak to the student in ways that are personally revelatory, psychologically meaningful, or spiritually profound. This goes beyond the ethical (if one can say such a thing) into other kinds of "truth." Consider, for example, Buber's comments about what "the man of today" must do in reading the Bible:

> He must face the Book with a new attitude as something new. He must yield to it, withhold nothing of his being, and let whatever will occur between himself and it. He does not know which of its sayings and images will overwhelm him and mold him, from where the spirit will ferment and enter into him, to incorporate itself anew in his body. But he holds himself open.[52]

What might Buber have in mind here? It is clear that there are models of interpretation that find ways of taking the texts of the Bible into the realm of personal or psychological meaning. One classic example is the way by which early Hasidism reinterpreted biblical texts in deeply personal ways. Gershom Scholem described this as the "process of spiritualization which biblical or rabbinic terms and concepts have undergone in Hasidic exegesis."[53] Scholem goes on to say that although this was not a novel idea in Hasidism, its "radical application, the hypertrophic use of this device" in this literature was remarkable. Classic concepts like Egypt, *galut* (exile), and *ge'ulah* (redemption)

were turned into allegorical catchwords denoting no longer only what they actually mean, but standing for a personal state of

mind, for amoral condition, or, as we would say in contemporary jargon, for existential situations of man. Notions like these
have lost their concrete historical or geographical meaning, they
have no longer to do with the fate and future of the nation but
with the individual's struggle for his own salvation.[54]

In this mode of interpretation, the Exodus from Egypt becomes
metaphorized into an expression of a person's personal redemption
from spiritual lethargy or sin. Even such a prosaic biblical passage as
"the servants of Isaac, digging in the valley, found a well of living waters" (Gen. 26:19) becomes an opportunity in early Hasidism for a per-
sonalized spiritual message:

> The patriarchs opened up the channels of mind in the world
> teaching all who were to come into the world how to dig within
> themselves a spring of living waters, to cleave to their fount, the
> root of their lives.[55]

Hasidism expresses itself in the language and modalities of an intact
religious culture. But even in a more secular era, such impulses can be
perceived. Michael Fishbane, a scholar of the Bible and its exegesis, has
tried to articulate what it might mean today for "an individual [to read]
texts in a wholly personal manner"[56] (later in the article quoted, he
deals with the "communal" dimension of reading texts), seeking to
make sense of a text traditionally deemed "sacred" in a more secular
age:

> Here, we may say, modern readers prowl around texts like
> wolves around Sinai—to paraphrase Kafka's well-known para-
> ble. Indeed we prowl around many texts, the Bible included,
> and wrest from these encounters fragments of various sorts. So
> viewed, we are, in part, a living texture of ideas derived from
> our reading. . . . Accordingly, the Bible may become sacred to us
> insofar as its images and language shape our discourse, stimu-
> late our moral and spiritual growth, and simply bind us to past
> generations which also took this text seriously. Indeed, the Bible
> may become sacred in this way because—together with other
> texts—it helps establish our personhood and outline our possi-
> bilities; and because it may provide the words and values
> through which we may cross over from the private to the inter-

human realm. No denial of death is this. It is rather a transcend-
ing of selfhood and its limitations through concourse with other
texts and other selves.[57]

The Bible in Fishbane's view, then—even in a secular time—becomes
"sacred" in a number of different ways. It provides a set of images and
words by which our own language and metaphoric substructures are
shaped. We lose our own "Gardens of Eden"; we wander years in our
wildernesses; we cast our bread upon the waters and hear the still, small
voice. It pushes us, in the manner of Nussbaum and Booth, toward
moral development. It helps elicit our own spiritual growth. And it links
us back across the generations to all those people who have lived and
died for this enduring text.
    What does it mean to say that studying the Bible helps "establish
our personhood and outline our possibilities"? In the Bible, we learn
new things, to be sure, but perhaps more important, we learn to see familiar things in a new way and rediscover truths that we had known before and forgotten. Gadamer points out, in the words of Georgia
Warnke, that "[i]nsofar as works of art are mimetic they are therefore
not only representational but pedagogical. In picking out certain features of their objects they teach their views or readers more of their objects than that audience previously understood. . . . On the one hand,
we learn from a work of art. . . . On the other, we recognize this new
way as something familiar, as something we knew or should have
known."[58]
    Proust's comments about the act of reading are equally true about
the experience of teaching and learning:

> In reality, every reader is, while he is reading, the reader of his
> own self. The writer's work is merely a kind of optical instru-
> ment which he offers to the reader to enable him to discern
> what, without this book, he would perhaps never have experi-
> enced in himself. And the recognition by the reader in his own
> self of what the book says is the proof of its veracity.[59]

The Bible offers teachers these potential rewards, these goals of
finding "truth," as they explore the biblical text. But the enumeration of
potential pedagogical goals, such as I have attempted to do in this chapter, does not bring the teacher's story to a close. Most of the great challenges are still ahead. In the next chapter, I will turn to the roadblocks

on the path, looking at ways that the lofty goals explored in this chapter may face their own complex difficulties.

Notes

1. Edward Greenstein, "Reading Strategies and the Story of Ruth," in *Women in the Hebrew Bible: A Reader,* ed. Alice Bach (New York & London: Routledge, 1999), pp. 211–31.
2. Stanley Fish, *Surprised by Sin: The Reader in* Paradise Lost (New York: St. Martin's, 1967).
3. Gail Zaiman Dorph, "What Do Teachers Need to Know to Teach Torah?" in *Essays in Education and Judaism in Honor of Joseph S. Lukinsky,* ed. Burton I. Cohen and Adina A. Ofek (New York: Jewish Theological Seminary, 2002), pp. 97–113.
4. Ibid., p. 104.
5. Also related is the reluctance of teachers to try anything out of the ordinary in their pedagogies. See David K. Cohen's discussion about the disincentives to implementing "adventurous teaching," in his "Teaching Practice: *Plus Que Ça Change,*" in *Contributing to Educational Change,* ed. Philip W. Jackson (Berkeley, Calif.: McCutchan, 1988). Also: Ann Lieberman and Lynne Miller, "The Social Realities of Teaching," in *Staff Development: New Demands, New Realities, New Perspectives,* ed. Ann Lieberman and Lynne Miller (New York: Teachers College Press, 1979); and Judith Warren Little, "Norms of Collegiality and Experimentation: Workplace Conditions of School Success," *American Educational Research Journal* 19, no. 3 (fall 1982): 325–40.
6. These ideas have been influenced by Seymour Fox, the person in Jewish education who has most systematically explored these ideas. See n. 14 to the introduction in this volume for references.
7. See Israel Scheffler's comments on the connection between philosophy and practice in his article "Philosophy and the Curriculum," in his *Reason and Teaching* (London: Routledge & Kegan Paul, 1973).
8. Israel Scheffler, "Justifying Curriculum Decisions," in *Reason and Teaching,* p. 119. For another aspect of justification, see Walter I. Ackerman, "Some Uses of Justification in Jewish Education," *AJS Review* 2 (1977): 116–25.
9. Eleanor Duckworth, *"The Having of Wonderful Ideas" and Other Essays on Teaching and Learning* (New York: Teachers College Press, 1987).
10. R. S. Peters, "The Justification of Education," in his *Education and the Education of Teachers* (London: Routledge & Kegan Paul, 1977), p. 96.
11. Ibid., p. 99.
12. Israel Scheffler, "In Praise of the Cognitive Emotions," *Teachers College Record* 79, no. 2 (December 1977): 171–86.
13. Joseph Schwab, "Eros and Education," in his collected essays, *Science, Curricu-*

lum, and Liberal Education, ed. Ian Westbury and Neil J. Wilkof (Chicago: University of Chicago Press, 1978), p. 109.

14. Peters, "The Justification of Education," p. 99.

15. I have discussed the notion of *Torah lishmah* previously, in my *Finding Our Way: Jewish Texts and the Lives We Lead Today* (New York: Schocken, 1990), pp. 211–16. For a extended presentation of many of these complexities, see Norman Lamm, *Torah Lishmah: Torah for Torah's Sake in the Works of Rabbi Hayyim of Volozhin and His Contemporaries* (Hoboken, N.J.: Ktav, 1989); for an important discussion of the implications of these ideas for education, see Michael Rosenak, *Roads to the Palace: Jewish Texts and Teaching* (Providence: Berghahn, 1995). The talmudic quotation appears in tractate Nedarim 62a.

16. R. S. Peters, *Ethics and Education* (New York: Scott, Foresman, 1966), p. 86.

17. Ibid., p. 100.

18. The relevance of Gadamer for religious education has been explored by a number of writers in recent years—in particular, articles by: Ernest Hass, "Practical Biblical Interpretation," *Religious Education* 88, no. 2 (spring 1993): 190–211; William Cutter, "Reading for Ethics—Renouncing Simplicity," *Religious Education* 88, no. 2 (spring 1993): 212–25; and Deborah Kerdemon, "Some Thoughts about Hermeneutics and Jewish Religious Education," *Religious Education* 93, no. 1 (winter 1998): 29–43.

19. Catherine H. Zuckert, *Postmodern Platos* (Chicago: University of Chicago Press, 1996), p. 90.

20. An interesting, but very different, approach to the question of "truth" in teaching has been raised by the literary scholar Robert Scholes in his book *The Rise and Fall of English* (New Haven: Yale University Press, 1998). Scholes is not so much concerned with the truth of texts in the lives of individuals but rather with the problem of teachers in making truth claims in an academic world of relativism. One of the reasons that professors in the humanities "feel bad," he says, "is that we have become reluctant to make claims of truth about the matters we teach. Powerful voices in our field have taught us to be embarrassed by the word *truth,* and thus either to avoid it or condemn it" (p. 39).

21. Hans-Georg Gadamer, *Truth and Method,* trans. Joel Weinsheimer and Donald G. Marshall, 2d rev. ed. (New York: Continuum, 1999), p. 166.

22. Georgia Warnke, *Gadamer: Hermeneutics, Tradition and Reason* (Stanford, Calif.: Stanford University Press, 1987), p. 14.

23. Gadamer, *Truth and Method,* p. 295.

24. Ibid., p. 294.

25. Harvey Siegel, "Teaching, Reasoning, and Dostoyevsky's *The Brothers Karamazov,*" in *From Socrates to Software: The Teacher as Text and the Text as Teacher,* ed. Philip W. Jackson and Sophie Haroutunian-Gordon, NSSE Yearbook, pt. 1 (Chicago: National Society for the Study of Education, 1989), p. 116.

26. Ibid., p. 131.

27. Ibid., p. 125.
28. Ibid.
29. Ibid., p. 129.
30. Ibid., p. 123.
31. Richard Rorty, *Contingency, Irony, and Solidarity* (Cambridge: Cambridge University Press, 1989), p. 141.
32. Ibid.
33. Ibid.
34. Martha Nussbaum, *Love's Knowledge: Essays on Philosophy and Literature* (Oxford: Oxford University Press, 1990), pp. 23–24.
35. Ibid., p. 22.
36. Ibid., p. 37.
37. Martha Nussbaum, *Poetic Justice* (Boston: Beacon, 1995), p. 2.
38. Ibid., p. 5.
39. Ibid., pp. 7, 9, and passim.
40. The Bible differs from other *ancient* texts as well—see Erich Auerbach's classic "Odysseus' Scar," in his *Mimesis* (Princeton: Princeton University Press, 1953), pp. 3–24. On how the Bible tells its stories, see, among many other possible sources: Meir Sternberg, *The Poetics of Biblical Narrative* (Bloomington: Indiana University Press, 1985); Joel Rosenberg, "Biblical Narrative," in *Back to the Sources: Reading the Classic Jewish Texts,* ed. Barry W. Holtz (New York: Simon and Schuster / Summit, 1984), pp. 31–82; and Robert Alter, *The Art of Biblical Narrative* (New York: Basic Books, 1981).
41. Edward L. Greenstein, "An Equivocal Reading of the Sale of Joseph," in *Literary Interpretations of Biblical Narratives,* ed. Kenneth R. R. Gros Louis with James S. Ackerman (Nashville: Abingdon, 1982), 2:114–25.
42. Nussbaum, *Love's Knowledge,* p. 36.
43. Sternberg, *The Poetics of Biblical Narrative.*
44. Nussbaum, *Love's Knowledge,* p. 37.
45. Mark Johnson, *Moral Imagination* (Chicago: University of Chicago Press, 1993), p. 196.
46. Alasdair MacIntyre, *After Virtue,* 2d ed. (Notre Dame, Ind.: University of Notre Dame Press, 1984), p. 216. The literature on "narrative" is immense—in literary criticism, anthropology, psychology, and education, among other disciplines. In education, one may look at Jerome Bruner's classic essay "Two Modes of Thought," in his *Actual Minds, Possible Worlds* (Cambridge: Harvard University Press, 1986), pp. 11–43; and Hunter McEwan and Kieran Egan, eds., *Narrative in Teaching, Learning, and Research* (New York: Teachers College Press, 1995).
47. Wayne C. Booth, *The Company We Keep: An Ethics of Fiction* (Berkeley: University of California Press, 1988). Booth has been an important influence on Martha Nussbaum. See her important review "Reading for Life," in *Love's Knowledge,* pp. 230–44.

48. Nussbaum, *Love's Knowledge*, p. 233.

49. Booth, *The Company We Keep*, p. 70.

50. Ibid., p. 71.

51. Ibid. p. 74.

52. Martin Buber, "The Man of Today and the Jewish Bible," in his collection *On the Bible*, ed. Nahum N. Glatzer (New York: Schocken, 1968), p. 5.

53. Gershom Scholem, "The Neutralization of Messianism in Early Hasidism," in his *The Messianic Idea in Judaism and Other Essays on Jewish Spirituality* (New York: Schocken, 1971), p. 200.

54. Ibid.

55. Menahem Nahum of Chernobyl, "Meor eyanim" (The light of the eyes), in *Upright Practices, The Light of the Eyes,* ed. and trans. Arthur Green (New York: Paulist, 1982), p. 189. See Green's introduction to that vol., esp. pp. 9–16, for more on the "personalizing" tendency in hasidic thought.

56. Michael Fishbane, *The Garments of Torah* (Bloomington: Indiana University Press, 1989), p. 132.

57. Ibid.

58. Warnke, *Gadamer,* p. 59.

59. Marcel Proust, *Time Regained (Remembrance of Things Past,* vol. 3), translated by C. K. Scott Moncrieff, Terence Kilmartin and Andreas Mayor (New York: Random House, 1981), p. 949.

CHAPTER FIVE
The Pedagogical Challenge of Difficult Texts

As a Bible teacher, I try to keep my eye both on the orientations that I wish to use and the larger goals that motivate my entire teaching enterprise. In the previous chapter, I looked at one of those overarching goals, one that I find particularly compelling in my own work—teaching the Bible with an eye toward "truth." I tried to examine different conceptions of truth, reflecting on some of the issues that emerge for me—or any teacher—in trying to teach from this perspective.

If we see the Bible as representing truth, of course, we will soon come face-to-face with certain biblical texts that disturb us, that force us to ask, What truth can be found here? These are difficult texts to teach, and every Bible teacher is likely to have his or her own personal collection of challenging passages. In this chapter, I want to examine the problem of difficult texts, asking why we as teachers find them hard to teach and exploring how we might think about our difficulties. The Bible is an old and "foreign" book, and part of our difficulty has to do with the way we approach any work from the distant past. To begin to address our questions, therefore, I want to go at things indirectly: before we turn to the Bible, let us look at a different "foreign" text and see the way that reflecting upon that text may help us think about teaching the Bible.

•   •   •

So we will begin with a story: in the middle of his life, a man loses his way. He sinks into a valley of despair; he becomes lost in a forest of confusion. He loses hope. He knows where he would like to go, but the way is difficult, filled with terrifying impediments. How can he find what he seeks? How can he reach the goal that lies, tantalizingly, before him? Suddenly, out of nowhere, someone comes to his aid—a guide, a *teacher* who can lead him. With his teacher's help, he begins his long journey.

Thus begins Dante's *Inferno,* a work that deals with nothing less than heaven and hell, the nature of sin, the ultimate consequences of human deeds, and the meaning of life and death. Yet parallel to these great themes, we see another story taking place as well. *The Inferno* is arguably the greatest representation in Western literature of the relationship between teacher and student, the most poignant portrait of what it means to learn and be taught.

What conception of teaching and learning do we see in *The Inferno?* To begin with, we understand that for the first-person poet-narrator of *The Inferno,* education is centered in a relationship with one particular teacher, the great Latin poet Virgil, who has returned from his own resting place in the outer ring of hell to guide our narrator through a terrifying excursion through the underworld. The purpose of the journey is not even clear—it begins with Dante[1] unable to reach his ultimate goal, to "ascend the delightful mountain, source/And principle that causes every joy" (1.59–60) because his way has been blocked by a terrible (and no doubt allegorical) she-wolf. Virgil proposes to take him on a journey, yet how the journey through hell will help him is not entirely obvious. At their first meeting, Virgil tells him, "A different path from this one would be best/For you to find your way from this feral place" (1.70–71), but as time passes, it becomes clear that the journey itself plays a crucial role in Dante's ability to make that ascent. The journey, in other words, is part of the redemptive process. Or, to put it in other terms: the experience of learning that will take place along the way is the reason for the journey. *The Inferno* is at once a story about the nature of education and a tale of a person being educated. "This is no causeless trek" (7.9), after all. Dante is not in hell "for punishment of guilt . . . but for experience" (28.44–45).

Experience. Dante's journey is about experience, but it is not about unmediated experience; it is about experience as refracted through the eyes of a teacher. Virgil's role is crucial for Dante's education, but how precisely that act of educating occurs is worth looking at more closely. Like most teachers, Virgil educates by speaking; indeed, his very essence seems linked to vocal expression. At their first meeting, the poet describes Virgil with a striking line, as "one who seemed nearly to fade/As though from long silence" (1.47–48). Without speech, he has virtually disappeared. And, in fact, throughout the rest of *The Inferno*, we see Virgil do a great deal of talking—lecturing, we might say—in his encounters with Dante. Curiously, unlike most teachers, however, Virgil rarely asks questions. He employs a different pedagogical method, one that seems in some ways strikingly modern: rather than asking his "student" questions, Virgil instead confronts him with experiences. These experiences in turn lead *Dante,* the student, to ask his teacher to interpret what he has just seen. "Who are these . . . ?" Dante (not Virgil) asks, and "What is this . . . ?" over and over again. At the beginning of canto 8, for example, they come upon two signal flames answering each other:

> I turned to face
> My sea of knowledge and said, O Master, say:
> What does this beacon mean? And the other fire—
> What answer does it signal? And who are they
> Who set it there? (8.6–10)

And the "sea of knowledge" will answer him. The pattern recurs numerous times throughout the poem. It is as if Virgil believes that it is only by looking at confusion face-to-face that Dante will be able to know enough or care enough to ask serious questions. Virgil is, in other words, a kind of "constructivist" teacher: he believes, it appears, that

> meaning and understanding are constructed in particular circumstances by individuals according to their distinctive conceptual and emotional biographies. One comes to know, in other words, by inventing understanding, and this invention involves an interaction of past knowledge with the experience of the moment. This constructivist perspective emphasizes the importance of direct experience and the gradual accumulation of knowledge structures from reflection on that experience over time.[2]

Part of what Dante learns is to become an asker of questions. He emulates his teacher (11.100) and the characteristic way of learning that Virgil propounds—through reflection on experience.

In addition to a constructivist approach (or perhaps because of that approach), *The Inferno* emphasizes the power of personal relationship as a core dimension of the teacher-learner experience. In the same canto quoted above, in a moment of terror, Dante calls out:

> "O my dear guide," I said,
> "Who has restored my confidence seven times over,
> And drawn me out of peril—stay at my side." (8.92–94)

And Virgil answers him, "[W]ait for me here/And feed your spirit hope and comfort: remember,/ I won't abandon you in this nether sphere" (8.100–101). This is a theme that runs throughout the poem, building in significance as time passes. Indeed, the personal connection between Dante and Virgil seems to be the core definition of the learning experience itself. Virgil comes to know the very core of Dante's being. "You," Dante tells him, "know the things I leave unsaid" (19.35). In fact, Virgil compares it to the ultimate image of inner interpersonal understanding, the relationship between parent and child. In canto 8, Virgil is a "gentle father" (line 103); later, he becomes a mother, protecting and rescuing her child:

> My leader took me up at once, and did
> As would a mother awakened by a noise
> Who sees the flames around her, and takes her child
> Concerned for him more than herself. (23.34–37)

This is what it means to be a teacher—to be the father or mother of the student, the originator of life itself. *The Inferno*, I have tried to indicate here, is a book about the acts of teaching and learning. It is, at least in part, about the relationship between the teacher and the student in an idealized setting; here, the student comes to leave behind the greatest pit of despair a human being can imagine and move on to maturity in the footsteps of his mentor. Following the pathway opened by the beloved teacher—"Following in the tracks of his dear feet" (23.148)—we find our liberation.

So goes *The Inferno*. But what, one might ask, have I been doing these last few pages? I have begun an exploration of the idea of teaching and learning using an old text as my guide. I have, we might say, played Dante to Dante, and he has played Virgil to me! From where may we learn wisdom? From a teacher, true, but in this case, from a text. But in what way can texts serve as teachers? In what ways can we legitimately use ancient texts for our own present-day purposes? And what difficulties do we confront in doing so?

As teachers of the Bible—or of Dante—these questions are always with us. They touch upon the core issues of our enterprise. Consider for a moment some of the key impediments we face in teaching *The Inferno*. To begin with, the text presents a cultural distance between us and itself. The book, for example, is rich in allusions to contemporary figures of Dante's time whom we no longer recognize. Vanna Fucci, Cianfa Donati, and Guido da Montefeltro are merely fine-sounding Italian syllables to us; to Dante and his contemporary readers, they were more than known figures—each had its own cultural valence. Alluding to these figures *meant* something. To us, they are at best footnotes in an annotated edition.

A similar problem obtains even in texts not half so old. Let us say, for example, that I wanted to teach Jane Austen's *Pride and Prejudice* (1813) to a class of high school students. Early on in the novel, in a discussion about Mr. Darcy, one character remarks, "I can guess how it was; every body says that he is ate up with pride, and I dare say he had heard somehow that Mrs. Long does not keep a carriage, and had come to the ball in a hack chaise." To understand this sentence, students would need to know the cultural significance of "carriage" and "hack chaise" in early-nineteenth-century England.[3] They would need to know that keeping a carriage was a sign of status and wealth, while hiring a hack meant that one belonged to a lower rung of the social ladder. In nineteenth-century England, such cultural nuances expressed important values in a code well understood by all. Certainly, readers of novels— the emerging middle class being particularly connected to this literature—would have interpreted these subtleties with ease. In *The Small House at Allington* (1864), a popular novel by Trollope, for example, the disastrous marriage of the bounder, Mr. Crosbie, and his harridan bride, Amelia, is symbolized by her continuous prattling, imploring him to keep a carriage and his continual denial of her wishes!

A second difficulty that the teacher faces in teaching these texts is philosophical distance. The milieu of ideas upon which *The Inferno* is based is very distant from us. To read the poem, we need to bridge the gap to a world that viewed hell as a living reality, that saw nine circles of inferno populated by the souls of actual beings. This is a profound gap, and interpreters have struggled since the advent of modernity with ways of overcoming it.[4]

Reading and teaching the Bible, too, confront us with examples of both cultural and philosophical distance. The Bible presents a conception of reality in which the very structure of the physical universe is different from our own. When the rains deluge the earth in Genesis, they emanate from *arubot,* "sluices," in a typical translation (Gen. 7:11), windows that open to let in the cosmic waters within which our world is more or less suspended.[5]

Beyond its conception of the physical world (its "science," we might say), the Bible confronts us with a reality in which ideas of causality and the divine challenge our own perspectives. When Abraham brings Isaac to be sacrificed in Genesis 22, Abraham's willingness to do so indicates that the patriarch has passed God's test. A modern reader may be considerably more ambivalent.[6] When God speaks to Job out of the whirlwind, we are even more confused about how to understand what the text is trying to tell us.[7]

From the point of view of the teacher, cultural distance is the easier problem to address. We can, in essence, "footnote" the lesson. We can explain allusions and explicate the cultural underpinnings of the texts that we teach. In the same way that we can tell English literature students about carriages, hacks, coaches, and traps—and the social distinctions that they imply—we can explain the social significance of the Levirate marriage or the importance of the Bible telling us that Saul came from the tribe of Benjamin and David from the tribe of Judah.

Nonetheless, even here we should be careful not to underestimate the pedagogic difficulties that face us, particularly when teaching children. A cultural allusion (in any culture) works through its essential immediacy. If I read a novel today that says, "After all that, he traded in his Taurus for a Mercedes convertible," we know what is implied—about class, about ambition, about pretension. True, as a teacher I can draw analogies from the automobiles of today to the horse-drawn vehicles in a nineteenth-century novel, but the layer of explanation undercuts the rapidity by which cultural allusions are grasped. A recent news report told of a judge in a small town who sentenced a noisemaking teenager to listen to 100 hours of Wayne Newton music over the course of a week. How could I explain the meaning of that punishment to a visitor from Sri Lanka, or even from London? Teachers of Bible are faced with similar distances. By the time the teacher is finished providing the footnotes, as it were, the point of the text may be lost. It is not unlike the experience of having to explain a joke to someone who doesn't get it at its first telling.

The issue of cultural distance also applies to the student's perception of the way the Bible is written. The devices employed by the text may make the text feel different from the literature that students generally read. This is particularly striking in narratives[8] in which typical features include the repetition of speech or events either directly or in less obvious ways. In doing so, the Bible creates a kind of intertextual experience for the aware reader, through which different parts of the text comment interpretively upon one another.[9] Commentators both ancient and contemporary have noticed the prevalence of these characteristic narrative devices, and part of the challenge of teaching the Bible is helping students both recognize and resonate with these dimensions of biblical storytelling.

Though cultural distance may present challenges for the teacher, philosophical distance is even more problematic. At least two kinds of problems are presented to the teacher: first, we find texts that are difficult because their point of view is just plain different from our own. The Bible has a symbol system and ideational framework that require explication and understanding. Its concepts of holiness, covenant, divinity, prophecy, and law are all very different from those of our contemporary world.

But the second type of philosophical gap is more disturbing. In the Bible, we encounter texts that go beyond "different," or unintelligible, into the realms of being bothersome, unpalatable, or even offensive to our contemporary sensibility. These are texts in which the moral perspective of the Bible is unacceptable, as judged by our own standards. What might "unacceptable" mean? A range of difficulties may be identified. There are texts that make the reader feel that the Bible is a harsh and brutal document, wrapped up in vengeance and violence: "The righteous man will rejoice when he sees revenge;/ he will bathe his feet in the blood of the wicked," says Ps. 58:11. Saul is punished for not executing Agag, king of Amalek, an act carried out by the prophet Samuel (1 Samuel 15). God hardens the heart of Pharaoh and then destroys the firstborn of Egypt in the Book of Exodus.

There are places in which the moral compass of the Bible feels askew to the modern reader: we see Jacob stealing his brother's blessing, Israel devastating the peoples of Canaan, violators of the Sabbath being put to death. Less violent, but disturbing nonetheless, are texts about the treatment of women and institutions such as slavery.

In what ways can the teacher deal with these difficult texts? Let me suggest five approaches that teachers may find helpful, five ways of thinking about difficult texts. I am going to focus particularly on difficulties arising out of what I have called philosophical distance because, as I've noted above, difficulties related to cultural distance—though challenging—are less difficult for teachers to negotiate.

First Approach: The Principle of Charity

The first approach is perhaps more of an attitude than it is a way of working. Namely, one goal that teachers need to work toward, it seems to me, is helping students de-emphasize their evaluative faculties, their desire to leap to judgment, and put more of a focus on understanding the texts that they study. In chapter 1, I wrote about the challenge of the contemporary American "milieu" to teaching the Bible. There I was interested in "American religion" (in the Emersonian sense that I explored in that chapter) and its impact on teaching sacred literature. Here I have in mind something else, though it, too, may be seen as a version of Robert Bellah's "Sheilaism," which we explored earlier. The "me-focus" of contemporary America and American spirituality is a version of the "culture of narcissism" that has been the topic of much discussion in recent years. Part of that narcissism is a focus on *my* reaction, and *my* likes and dislikes. This is true in the marketplace and has become equally true in the world of ideas. As teachers, we see students (of all ages—adults, too, certainly) whose first reaction upon seeing any piece of literature, particularly something distant from themselves, is to talk about *their* reactions to the text. What we see is a kind of intellectual consumerism in which the customer is always right. It is an ailment that the literary scholar Eugene Goodheart has characterized as the situation in which

> if the classic does not speak to our immediate concerns, then it can make no urgent claim on our attention. We make a classic relevant by projecting our interests into the work. Every reading becomes a reading of ourselves.[10]

In place of this kind of attitude, wouldn't it be possible for teachers to lead students away from judgment and toward a kind of humility before the text? As Goodheart puts it, "A reader may decide that a particular classic is not for him, that it is deficient in rewards—not, however, before the work has been given a chance. Its alienness should not be a mark against it."[11]

This approach would, in short, mean trying to help students learn to read ancient texts like the Bible in the spirit of the "principle of charity," a notion associated with the philosopher Willard Quine.[12] For our purposes, Quine's concept has been usefully explicated (and enlarged) by the Israeli philosopher and Judaica scholar Moshe Halbertal.[13] Halbertal goes beyond Quine's original conception of merely "shedding light" on a confusing statement or text so that the text does not appear to be meaningless. Halbertal uses the principle of charity to mean that a text can be "read in the 'best' possible light in order to redeem it."[14] Halbertal draws upon Ronald Dworkin's use and extension of Quine's ideas in legal theory and applies the principle of charity to questions about the nature of the traditional Jewish canon as it has been understood in Jewish history. I, in turn, would like to take Halbertal's use of the principle of charity and see how it might apply to the pedagogical problems we have been looking at here.

Let us first look at what Halbertal has accomplished and then see the way that it might apply to pedagogy. Halbertal wants to consider what it might mean to take ideas about how judges operate in interpreting laws "in the best possible light" (Dworkin's concern) and apply those ideas to looking at Jewish texts—particularly the Bible—and how they have been interpreted. As Halbertal points out, the situation in thinking about a sacred text is complicated by the fact that in this case, unlike with secular legal materials, the Bible traditionally has been viewed as a text in which

> the speaker is God and [the text] is thus by definition perfect; not only can no contradictions exist but the text is the best possible. . . . Reading a holy text requires using the principle of charity as generously as possible in interpreting it, since it is inconceivable that such a text could err. . . . In the case of the Scriptures, there is an a priori interpretive commitment to show the text in the best possible light. . . . The more canonical a text, the more generous its treatment.[15]

But what happens when we find ourselves in conflict with what the text says? Halbertal shows that that issue is an old and complicated one in Jewish intellectual history. He brings as an example Maimonides' discussion of what would happen if what he believed to be true from (here I use a somewhat anachronistic term) a "scientific" point of view conflicted with the teachings of Scriptures. Such an issue would be, for example, the question of whether the world was created or eternal. "Maimonides," Halbertal notes, "states that if it were clear to him in a metaphysical sense that in truth the world was eternal rather than created, he would interpret the Scriptures in harmony with this truth."[16] And indeed, Halbertal shows, Maimonides did apply this interpretive principle in his work. In the conflict between science and Scripture, resolution comes through interpreting the text, not by rejecting the scientific truth.

Halbertal shows that the Maimonidean position is not the only approach found in the Jewish interpretive tradition: "Maimonides' view that a holy text necessitates maximal charity in its interpretation is opposed by [a different traditional] view that a holy text must be interpreted with minimal charity."[17] Ironically, "minimal charity" is seen as a necessity (according to this view) in order to preserve the ultimate authority of the sacred text:

> According to the radical approach, it is the text that must determine the interpreter's concept of charity. He cannot postulate a conception of justice or truth that he formulated before his encounter with the text and still interpret the text in the best possible light. The holiness and authority of the text is so all-encompassing that it alone determines the concepts of good and evil, truth and falsity; no other criterion exists by which it can be interpreted.[18]

From a pedagogical perspective, the teacher today might well lean toward Maimonides' "moderate" position concerning interpretive charity, from two different vantage points. First, in keeping with the moderate view, students can deal with difficult texts as Maimonides does—through a strategy of interpretation, modifying perhaps the original intent of the text to make sense in a contemporary world. Second, as I have suggested earlier, the principle of charity plays another role as well—the need to teach students a kind of respect for the text. Perhaps the model should be that we treat the text as a wise older relative—it is true that we might disagree with what the elder says, but we must at least listen carefully before judging.

Second Approach:
Using the Classical Commentators

Second, from the teacher's point of view it is helpful to remember that at least some of the difficulties that we encounter in biblical sources were also viewed as problematic by commentators in the past. One strategy in dealing with these difficult texts, therefore, is to explore with students the ways that the Jewish hermeneutic tradition dealt with these same matters. So, for example, consider how one might teach Genesis 27, the episode in which Jacob pretends to be his brother, Esau, and in doing so deceives his blind father, Isaac, and steals the blessing intended for Esau. How might a teacher deal with the moral difficulties associated with Jacob's actions? Turning to traditional exegesis may help us discover some insights. For example, by looking at a recent article by the Bible scholar David Marcus, the teacher can discover various interpretations offered by the classical Jewish commentators on this story. Marcus shows two main tendencies in the interpretative tradition,

> one holding that the deception was not justified while the other held that it was. Those who acknowledged that the deception was wrong offered a moral interpretation or attempted to shift the blame from Jacob to Rebecca or even to Isaac himself.[19]

Jacob, according to some interpreters of the first tendency, "did deceive his father but he was punished for his deception later in life,"[20] particularly in the story of Jacob and Laban. Others, such as Josephus, saw Rebecca as the main culprit in the story, letting Jacob off the hook, but still viewing the text through a moral lens. An even more complex view, raised by the medieval commentators David Kimchi (twelfth–thirteenth century) and Samuel Ben Meir ("Rashbam," eleventh–twelfth century), saw Isaac himself as deeply involved in the incident, making the "deception" either not a deception at all but a duping of Esau or viewing the deception as self-deception, Isaac believing what he subconsciously wanted to believe about what was going on.[21]

At the same time, a different interpretive approach denies that there was any moral wrong in the deception at all; rather, this view justifies what Jacob did either on the legal grounds that the sale of the birthright

by Esau in Genesis 25 had given Jacob rights to the blessing, or by arguing in theological terms that "the blessing had already been prenatally
promised by God to Jacob when Rebecca consulted the oracle."[22] Such
arguments, Marcus points out, can be found in David Kimchi and in
Ibn Ezra (twelfth century), among others.

The teacher who turns to traditional commentators such as these
has a number of advantages. This approach gives students a sense of
connection to an interpretive tradition in which they become participants. It helps students recognize some of the enduring dilemmas of biblical studies and allows them to see that raising such questions—as they
themselves may have done—should not disconnect them from the tradition, but may in fact link them to that tradition.

Nonetheless, we should also recognize that this approach to problematic texts has very specific shortcomings that cannot be underestimated. First, the kinds of problems that the classical commentators raise
may, at times, differ from those that students today will raise. The case
about stealing the blessing, explored above, is an example of the tradition being troubled by an issue that a contemporary reader may also
find bothersome. Other problems that students might raise (such as the
role of women in certain biblical texts) are less likely to be discovered in
the commentators. We may be delighted to find examples of such concerns in the tradition, but intellectual honesty will require us to note
that such examples may be the exception rather than the rule.[23]

Beyond the issue of the problems that the commentators may have
found in the text, we also encounter difficulties with the specific
answers that they give. In the case above, for instance, the second
approach to the text essentially argues that "the goal justifies the
means."[24] For teachers to use commentaries that justify immoral behavior on these grounds is likely to raise considerable difficulties. And even
if one could negotiate those tricky waters (for example, an adroit
teacher could use this case as an opportunity to discuss the larger moral
issue—are there ever times in which the goals justify the means?), we
are in the position of essentially taking an attitude of defensive apolo-
getics vis-à-vis the biblical texts. Classical commentaries are an important resource. They help us understand the way that the Bible was
understood in the past and can offer many opportunities to rethink
problematic biblical texts in different ways, but they are not necessarily
going to help the teacher out of the dilemma of teaching challenging
texts.

Teachers sometimes run into a different kind of problem when using traditional commentaries to elucidate the Bible. These commentaries are themselves products of a particular milieu and intellectual framework. Reading the Bible through the eyes of classic midrashic or medieval interpreters may get the teacher entangled in questions of what the Bible is trying to say versus what the commentator is seeing in the Bible. Of course, such a conflict may be seen either as a dilemma or a strength, depending on one's overarching goals for teaching the Bible. If your goal is to help students learn to uncover the historical and contextual meaning of the text, then "intrusions" from later commentators may be unwelcome. Historical scholars of the Bible, for example, point out that the notion of an eternal soul and therefore a division between body and soul is not a biblical notion (at least in the vast majority of the Bible). According to this view, later biblical commentators, influenced by Greek culture, read this idea into the biblical text.[25] The teacher working on the opening of Genesis would have to consider if he or she read *nefesh hayya* as (in the King James version of Gen. 2:7) "man became a living *soul*" or as (in the NJPS) "man became a living *being.*"

Others may not view the use of later commentary as an intrusion at all. James Kugel, in particular, has argued that later commentary is inextricably bound up with the Bible; indeed, the Bible *becomes* the Bible when it is read through the eyes of the ancient commentators. Through most of the past hundred years, Kugel says, Bible scholars failed "to take into account the crucial role played by ancient interpreters in the very emergence of the Bible":[26]

> The activity of ancient biblical interpreters was a—perhaps *the*—striking instance of how interpretation is inevitably a kind of second authorship. It was *their* Bible, and no ragtag collection of ancient Near Eastern texts, that was canonized in the closing centuries of the Second Temple period, and their Bible is, to an extent with which all who love God's word must reckon, ours today.[27]

From the point of view of pedagogy, Kugel's view would argue strongly for the use of traditional commentary as an important—indeed, necessary—component of teaching biblical texts. But it would not, as I have indicated above, necessarily solve the problem of problematic texts.

Third Approach: To Explain, Not to Defend

The third approach is represented by the distinguished Bible scholar Moshe Greenberg in an article written over forty years ago.[28] It is, to my mind, still the best articulation of a role for the teacher that we might call "dispassionate explainer" of the Bible's point of view:

> It order to carry out his duty the teacher is not required to assent personally to the answers given by the Bible, or to the manner in which it deals with the issues it raises. He may have a different viewpoint, or he may not yet have reached sure ground in his own mind on these matters. This does not disqualify him from teaching. For the basic requirement of a Bible teacher is not faith, but understanding; not assent, but recognition of the profound issues of which the Bible treats.[29]

Greenberg's view, unlike what one may see in typical traditional commentaries, does not seek to defend the Bible; rather, he is interested in taking seriously the "profound issues" that lie behind the biblical text. The teacher, says Greenberg, does not need to agree with what the Bible presents, but the teacher "must comprehend [the Bible] thoroughly enough to make clear the problems that have agitated the faith in question, and to give the color of plausibility to the solutions it has found."[30]

Greenberg's view emanates out of two important assumptions, both with serious implications for biblical pedagogy. First is his view of the ultimate goal of teaching the Bible, specifically to students younger than those in university courses. Greenberg sees the task of Bible teachers as

> to convey the religious significance of the Bible, and they can do this only after having gotten hold of the great spiritual issues that animate it. This means that they must go beyond what usually constitutes biblical studies in colleges and seminaries.[31]

Unlike university scholars "who can content themselves with the Bible as literature or archaeology without responsibility for its religious teaching,"[32] the teacher must be able to present the Bible's religious message as convincingly and powerfully as possible, without acting as a defensive apologist for the material on the one hand or as a proselytizer on the other.

For Greenberg, the key is placing the Bible before the students and *letting the Bible speak for itself*. It is not the teacher's job to take the student to the next level, to religious commitment. "The step beyond [presenting the Bible as best as can be done], from understanding to conviction and faith, must be left to the effect of the material itself."[33] Greenberg has a great deal of confidence in the power of the Bible to operate on the student's soul as long as the teacher does his or her job well. Greenberg's position frees the teacher from a kind of "clerical" burden, we might say, but it is a demanding role nonetheless. It is far more challenging than the university scholar's situation. As he puts it, quite movingly:

> The one commitment that may be fairly expected of a teacher of Bible is to the contemplative and reflective life. This commitment is sufficient, is indeed a warrant—the only possible warrant—that his teaching will not be trivial. This much may be expected of the teacher, since it is in the hope that his students will themselves be directed toward making a similar commitment that they have been entrusted to him.[34]

Greenberg has laid out a serious challenge about what it means to be a teacher of Bible. He goes beyond the problem of how to deal with difficult texts to look at the underlying goals of the entire enterprise. What is the "orientation" presented here? It is squarely in the camp of Bible as a religious text meant to speak to the lives of contemporary people, what we called the "personalization" approach in chapter 3. The means by which the teacher is to accomplish this goal have nothing to do with simplifying, missionizing, or manipulating either students or the text. It centers on understanding, and Greenberg believes that the text itself, well presented by the "contemplative" teacher, will be able to work its own magic.

Fourth Approach: The Strangeness of the Text

Earlier, we mentioned Eugene Goodheart's discussion of contemporary attitudes toward reading and literary scholarship. Goodheart criticizes Garry Wills's argument that the fundamental characteristic of a classic is "its capacity to renew itself in every age." This concept, according to Goodheart, weakens the power of the classic, since it "dissolves its core identity, so that it becomes whatever its readers wish to make it."[35] What Goodheart argues, in fact, is that the very quality that readers—particularly teachers and students—find difficult about "classics" is what they should be embracing! What makes the classic hard is what matters most:

> [A] classic may resist the interests and fashions of the age, even offend against them, and yet persist in being lively to us because of the imagination, intelligence, and force of the resistance. . . . The resistance forces us to examine what we have perhaps repressed in ourselves. . . . A classic does not necessarily convert us to its form of wisdom, but if it possesses the power implied by its status in the culture, it forces us to think about our resistance to it and to strengthen or overcome that resistance.[36]

The teacher's approach to the Bible would be to use the flip side of the "principle of charity," something we might call "the principle of strangeness." As Goodheart puts it:

> If education is a discovery of things one doesn't already know, we should not be looking in the works we read for a reflection of our own already formed understandings. If we do so, we may never hear the voices that speak a language that addresses our convictions in unfamiliar ways and perhaps unsettles them. . . .
>
> The reader who approaches a work with the aim of demystifying it is quite different from the open reader who may be discovering himself in the strangeness of the classic.[37]

The teacher, following this approach, would push students to confront the biblical text in all its alienness. Students would need to take the point of view seriously and ask what that text might demand of the listener who really embraces its concerns.

Fifth Approach: Gadamer's "Genetic" Alternative

But, perhaps, sometimes the strangeness is just too strange. What about those times in which we need to reject a text, where the variety of strategies outlined above won't work? One obvious approach to this situation is simply to ignore the text that creates the difficulties. Clearly, teachers have been doing this for many years, whether it means skipping over the bawdy language in *Hamlet* or the Judah and Tamar episode in Genesis 38. Such an approach is not to be scoffed at—as teachers, we are always editing what we teach, mostly in the interest of accommodating to the amount of time that we have, or more often, *don't* have. Except perhaps in the most advanced graduate studies, all teachers pick and choose within a broader potential curriculum, and one approach to difficult texts is to skip what is problematic.

Of course, such an answer may seem to be intellectually dishonest. We might even misrepresent the Bible itself in doing so. And we give ourselves too easy an out to take this route. To confront the Bible's "strangeness," we must really confront it.

There is perhaps another approach that takes a middle position, one that has been suggested by a thinker whom we investigated in chapter 4, Hans-Georg Gadamer.[38] Gadamer, as we saw, is concerned with the truth claims of the texts we read (and teach). In ways similar to those expressed above by Goodheart, Gadamer believes: "It is essential to grant to the text one is studying a certain normative authority, for it is only by doing so that one can test the adequacy of one's views about either the text or the issue on which it focuses.[39]

But much as we may want to confront the "truth" of the traditional text, there are times that such attempts will be unavailing. There are times that we will not be able to either hear or accept what that text is telling us. Here Gadamer offers his own approach to the problematic text: "When we read a text we always assume its completeness, and only when this assumption proves mistaken—i.e., the text is not intelligible—do we begin to suspect the text and try to discover how it can be remedied."[40] In such cases, another strategy—a different pedagogic approach—is called for:

> [T]he attempt to understand the truth of a work of art or the challenge it presents to one's own views has to *guide* the process of interpretation—otherwise there is no way of evaluating one's own or someone else's understanding of the work's meaning. . . . Still, this attempt to understand in the primary sense of understanding truth can fail and when it does one may have to be content with a genetic understanding of the conditions under which the claims could appear to be true.[41]

The notion expressed here is that an appeal to "genetic understanding" is a kind of last-resort effort to find meaning in the text. "Genetic" would mean exploring the context in which the biblical text originally appeared in an attempt not to justify the text in question but to view it sympathetically within the context of its own times. Here a turn to historical biblical scholarship would be the obvious move.

For Gadamer, it appears, such an approach is a kind of court of last resort for the text. At heart, the job of interpretation is to deal with the truth of the text, as we may experience it and as tradition has understood the text. Gadamer's views would lean toward the previously mentioned approach of appealing to traditional interpreters and of personal meaning-making, but there is a role for historical, contextual work in Gadamer's view as well. By such means, texts can be redeemed and rescued from obscurity.

•   •   •

Let us look at where we have come up to this point. I began this chapter by looking at Dante's *Inferno* as an example of a classic text and suggested ways in which that text might be read as an exploration about the nature of teachers and students. This reading led us to a consideration of the whole question of the use of "old" texts for contemporary purposes and from there to a close examination of difficulties that may be raised by the use of such texts, particularly texts that seem "problematic" to contemporary readers or students. I suggested five different approaches to thinking about or dealing with such difficulties.

"Problematic" texts in and of themselves, however, are not the only issue raised by the use of old texts like Dante or the Bible for contemporary purposes. The very act of using such texts raises problems. The contemporary philosopher of Jewish education Michael Rosenak has written at some length about the problem of what is sometimes called "educational translation":

When we observe what pedagogues do with subject matter that they are transmitting to pupils we see that translation is a staple of most educational activities and situations. For example, when teachers take pupils for an overnight hike to teach them scouting, they tell the youngsters that "we are going to have a great time." This is a didactically based translation of an exercise in social training and the inculcation of skills. When physicists assist in translating the substance of their subject matter into teaching models, or Biblical scholars help educators move scholarship into teaching Torah, they are likewise translating from scholarship to the classroom. Thus, any translation is an attempt, usually by an expert, to render a concept located in a mode of discourse that is incomprehensible to particular hearers, because they don't know it or don't take it seriously, into an idiom that does make sense to them and evokes interest in them, so that they are enabled to learn something from the (original) concept.[42]

It has been argued that the issue of "translation" is particularly problematic when trying to relate religious concepts to a secular context. Thus, Alasdair MacIntyre notes that

when secular predicates such as "powerful" and "wise" are transferred to a religious application, they undergo a change. Certainly they are used analogically; but just this is the point. A new element is introduced with the analogical adaptation of the concept. The transition from "powerful" to "omnipotent" is not merely quantitative. For the notion of "supreme in this or that class" cannot easily be transferred to a being who does not belong to a class (as God does not). And thus a new concept has been manufactured.[43]

Although Rosenak warns against the distortions that can happen in the act of educational translation, he has nonetheless argued for the viability of what he calls "partial translation":

The practitioner of partial translation insists that such a reflective yet deeply embedded cultural-religious world-view as the Jewish one can be expressed in varied literary or philosophical modes without sacrificing its character and authenticity.[44]

Exploring Dante for ideas about teaching is a kind of partial translation. We do so with an awareness that everything that I see in Dante might not have been seen or intended by Dante himself, that I am self-consciously interpreting for my own (contemporary) purposes, but that nonetheless the text before us has power and wisdom to offer a student today.

What is true of Dante is even more true of the Bible, a work of greater antiquity whose origins are embedded in mystery. The Bible carries with it, as well, the mystique of its own interpretive history, something that virtually no "secular" work can claim. Because through most of its history, the Bible has been viewed as sacred, because it has accrued centuries of exegesis from a variety of traditions, its hold on us is deep and difficult to characterize. It is simply *there*.

Franz Rosenzweig expressed this well when he wrote about the way that the Bible can speak to an ordinary contemporary person, a person who "is no believer, but no unbeliever either," one who "has neither belief nor unbelief, but both belief and unbelief happen to him":[45]

> A person leading such a life can bring to the Bible only a readiness both for belief and for unbelief, not a circumscribable belief that he finds the Bible confirming. Even his readiness is uncircumscribed and unlimited. Everything can become credible for him, even the incredible. What is believable is for him not interspersed within what is unbelievable—i.e., what merits unbelief—like veins of metal in stone, nor linked with its opposite like the kernel of the ear of corn with its dry husk. Rather, as a spotlight brings one sector of the landscape out of darkness, then another, then is dimmed, so for this person the days of his life illuminate Scripture, and let him see sometimes, amidst Scripture's human traits, also what is more than human—today here, tomorrow there, but with today's event implying no guarantee of tomorrow's. Yet everywhere these human traits can, in the light of a lived day become transparent, so that suddenly they are written into the center of his own heart, and the divinity in what has been humanly written is, for the duration of this heartbeat, as clear and certain as a voice calling in this moment into his heart and being heard. Not everything in Scripture belongs to him, not today and not ever. But he knows that he belongs to all of it. This readiness and this readiness alone is, as applied to Scripture, his belief.[46]

Rosenzweig speaks of readiness, and Gadamer argues for the "truth" of the text. But all these concerns may seem very far away indeed from the work that a teacher must do, in day school or synagogue classrooms with children, in universities with college-age students, or in

Bible study groups with adults. In what ways are we able to move from these theoretical investigations to the world of practice? How might the concerns that we have examined in this book find their way into programs that prepare teachers or efforts to work with teachers who are already in the field? This question will be our concern in the next chapter.

Notes

1. I am using the marvelous translation by Robert Pinsky, *The Inferno of Dante* (New York: Farrar, Straus & Giroux, 1994). For the sake of convenience and following convention, I will from this point forward refer to the narrator of the poem as "Dante" rather than "the speaker" or "the narrator." The poem is written in the first person, and the speaker is a poet located in a particular time (around 1300) and place (Florence). Of course, we might actually talk about two Dantes: Dante Alighieri (1265–1321), the author of the poem; and "Dante," the fictional narrator whom the reader encounters in the narrative. Though, as John Freccero has noted, "Unlike Plato's allegories, however, Dante's journey is autobiographical. Several passages are explicitly so and serve to reinforce the sense in which the descent into Hell may be thought of as a descent into Dante's past" (foreword to the Pinsky translation, p. xiv).

2. Walter Doyle, "Themes in Teacher Education Research," in *Handbook of Research on Teacher Education,* ed. W. Robert Houston (New York: MacMillan, 1990), p. 17. See also John D. Bransford, Ann L. Brown, and Rodney R. Cocking, eds., *How People Learn* (Washington, D.C.: National Academy Press, 1999).

3. See R. W. Chapman, ed., "On Carriages and Travel," in *Pride and Prejudice,* vol. 3 of *The Novels of Jane Austen* (London: Oxford University Press, 1988), pp. 560–84.

4. See, for example, Erich Auerbach's *Mimesis* (Princeton: Princeton University Press, 1953).

5. Nahum M. Sarna, *Understanding Genesis* (New York: Melton Research Center and Schocken, 1966).

6. Note Ruth Zielenziger's advice to teachers: "Not every interpretation of the text is admissible or valid. An interpretation is not acceptable if it violates either the content of the text or the reality of the biblical cultural milieu. For example, one may not interpret that Abraham failed the text in Genesis 22 . . . since the text contradicts this statement in Gen. 22:16." In her *Genesis: A New Teacher's Guide,* 3d ed. (New York: Melton Research Center, 1991), p. ix.

7. See the interesting presentation by Edward L. Greenstein, "In Job's Face/Facing Job," in *The Labour of Reading: Desire, Alienation, and Biblical Interpretation,* ed. Fiona C. Black, Roland Boer, and Erin Runions (Atlanta: Society of Biblical Literature, 1999), pp. 301–17.

8. For a brief overview, see Joel Rosenberg, "Biblical Narrative," in *Back to the Sources: Reading the Classic Jewish Texts,* ed. Barry W. Holtz (New York: Summit/Simon and Schuster, 1984), pp. 37–51.

9. See the discussions in, for example: Michael Fishbane, *Biblical Interpretation in Ancient Israel* (Oxford: Clarendon, 1985); George W. Savran, *Telling and Retelling: Quotation in Biblical Narrative* (Bloomington: Indiana University Press, 1988); Yair Zakovitch, *Through the Looking Glass: Reflection Stories in the Bible* [in Hebrew] (Tel Aviv: Hakibbutz Hameuchad, 1995).

10. Eugene Goodheart, *Does Literary Studies Have a Future?* (Madison: University of Wisconsin Press, 1999), p. 49.

11. Ibid., p. 51.

12. Willard V. Quine, *Word and Object* (Cambridge: MIT Press, 1960).

13. Moshe Halbertal, *People of the Book* (Cambridge: Harvard University Press, 1997).

14. Ibid., p. 27.

15. Ibid., p. 29.

16. Ibid.

17. Ibid., p. 30.

18. Ibid.

19. David Marcus, "Traditional Jewish Responses to the Question of Deceit in Genesis 27," in *Jews, Christians, and the Theology of the Hebrew Scriptures,* ed. Alice Ogden Bellis and Joel Kaminsky (Atlanta: Society of Biblical Literature, 2000), p. 295.

20. Ibid.

21. Ibid., pp. 296–99 and passim.

22. Ibid., p. 302.

23. For more on this issue, see my discussion of a midrashic response to the rivalry between Rachel and Leah: "Midrash and Modernity: Can Midrash Serve a Contemporary Religious Discourse?" in *The Uses of Tradition,* ed. Jack Wertheimer (New York: Jewish Theological Seminary, 1992), pp. 377–91.

24. Marcus, "Traditional Jewish Responses," p. 303.

25. See the classic discussion in Johannes Pedersen, *Israel: Its Life and Culture,* 4 vols. (London: Oxford University Press, 1926–40), and the note on Gen. 2:7, *nefesh hayya,* in Harry M. Orlinsky, ed., *Notes on the New Translation of the Torah* (Philadelphia: Jewish Publication Society, 1970), pp. 59–60.

26. James L. Kugel, *The Bible As It Was* (Cambridge, Mass.: Belknap Press of Harvard University Press, 1997), p. 558.

27. Ibid., p. 560.

28. Moshe Greenberg, "On Teaching the Bible in Religious Schools," *Jewish Education* 29, no. 3 (1959): 45–53.

29. Ibid., p. 45.

30. Ibid.

31. Ibid., pp. 45–46.

32. Ibid., p. 45.
33. Ibid., p. 46.
34. Ibid.
35. Goodheart, *Does Literary Studies Have a Future?* p. 50.
36. Ibid.
37. Ibid., pp. 51, 53.
38. For more on Gadamer and religious education, see n. 18 in chap. 4 of this volume.
39. Georgia Warnke, *Gadamer: Hermeneutics, Tradition and Reason* (Stanford, Calif.: Stanford University Press, 1987), p. 87.
40. Ibid.
41. Ibid., p. 89.
42. See Michael Rosenak, *Roads to the Palace: Jewish Texts and Teaching* (Providence: Berghahn, 1995), pp. 98–99.
43. Alasdair MacIntyre, "Is Understanding Religion Compatible with Believing?" in *Rationality*, ed. Bryan R. Wilson (Oxford: Oxford University Press, 1970), p. 63.
44. Rosenak, *Roads to the Palace*, p. xiv.
45. Franz Rosenzweig, "Scripture and Luther," in Martin Buber and Franz Rosenzweig, *Scripture and Translation*, trans. Lawrence Rosenwald with Everett Fox (Bloomington: Indiana University Press, 1994), p. 58.
46. Ibid., pp. 58–59.

CHAPTER SIX
And Now . . . to Teach

This book has been an attempt to help Jewish educators—Bible teachers, in particular—think more clearly about what they do. I have tried to explore two fundamental questions that a Bible teacher must face: What are my goals, and how shall I organize the knowledge of Bible that I have? In doing so, I have tried to look at these issues through a variety of lenses, considering the milieu in which teaching occurs, the orientations that help make sense of the subject matter, the overarching purposes behind our work, and the challenges that certain biblical texts present for the teacher today. It is clear that the issues of knowledge of the subject matter and goals for teaching are bound up with one another in close and almost inextricable ways. Throughout, I have tried to indicate some of the intellectual issues at the heart of this pursuit.

It might perhaps be argued that these foci are too theoretical, that they don't relate to the practical problems of teachers in classrooms. But in the spirit of Kurt Lewin's famous adage "there is nothing so practical as a good theory," I think it is important to look at these matters more carefully. Teachers without theory—whether that be articulated or even implicit—are working at a great disadvantage, both to themselves and to their students. As I have suggested in the introduction to this book, it is in theory that all practice is rooted, and it is in practice that all theory is tested. The process, ultimately, is interactive.

Because of its centrality to the issues of pedagogy, philosophers of education have long been interested in the relationship between theory and practice. Dewey, for example, worried that teacher-training institutions tended to put far too much emphasis on the *practices* of teaching while ignoring both deep engagement with the content of learning and the principles that need to undergird pedagogy. "There is a technique of teaching," he wrote, "just as there is a technique of piano-playing. The technique, if it is to be educationally effective, is dependent upon principles. But it is possible for a student to acquire outward form of method without capacity to put it to genuinely educative use."[1] It is this failure to integrate theory and practice that leads, in Dewey's view, to some teachers starting off strong in their teaching careers but eventually failing to grow. "Such persons," he says, "seem to know how to teach, but they are not students of teaching."[2] For teachers, "the root of the matter is not in them, unless they continue to be students of subject-matter and students of mind-activity."[3] By "mind-activity," Dewey meant what we would call the psychology of learning and perhaps even the psychology of learning particular subject matters, anticipating in these words Lee Shulman's concept of "pedagogical content knowledge."[4]

Many years ago, Philip Jackson used the terms "preactive" and "interactive" to define the two fundamental domains of a teacher's activities: "What the teacher does vis-à-vis students could be called 'interactive teaching' and what he does at other times—in an empty classroom, so to speak—could be called 'preactive teaching.'"[5] Most of Jackson's *Life in Classrooms* was concerned with the interactive side of teaching. In *this* book, on the other hand, I have dealt almost exclusively with the preactive dimension. Most scholars of education like to believe—as do I—that the preactive has, or can have, a great impact on the interactive (a point, perhaps, insufficiently noted by Jackson). Good planning does make a difference. In what ways can planning be enhanced? How might teachers of Bible do a better job of thinking in advance about what they are doing?

One way of thinking about this issue is to consider the steps needed to move from knowledge of subject matter to the act of teaching.[6] Sharon Feiman-Nemser and Margret Buchmann have called this the development of "pedagogical thinking," "thinking about how to build bridges between one's own understanding and that of one's students."[7] As I have indicated earlier in this book, the relationship between knowledge and teaching is complex, and contemporary ways of thinking about this issue have shown how interrelated these domains are.[8] By contrast, consider the "old" model. In that view, teaching might be represented as follows:

The Relationship between Subject Matter and Teaching

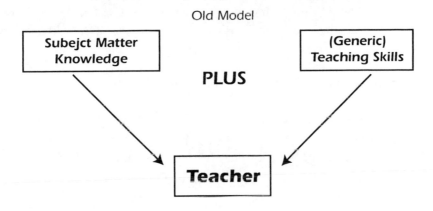

Old Model

Subejct Matter Knowledge

(Generic) Teaching Skills

PLUS

Teacher

Here teachers need first to "know" their subject matter (literature, mathematics, Bible, etc.) and then to learn a set of generic teaching skills. These latter skills might include knowing how to organize the seating in a classroom, understanding how to move from the simple to the complex in organizing learning activities, and knowing ways of treating students respectfully and consistently. These skills could be applied to any teaching situation. They are truly generic. I would need to know them if I were teaching relativity or teaching horseback riding. In the old model, the focus in teacher education was on those skills; the subject matter was learned elsewhere.

This model, adjusted for time and place, was the standard approach to preparing teachers in many institutions; indeed, it remains standard even today:

> As teacher education is currently organized, prospective teachers do practicums and student teaching, but these experiences are rarely supervised by the same people who teach courses. Subject matter content courses are distinct from methods courses and are usually taught outside of professional preparation programs. There is little institutional support for making

the connections between what it means to understand a subject
and how it can be taught and learned.[9]

But what this model misses is a different understanding of knowledge.
This old model resembles the view expressed in a wonderful little inter-
change toward the end of Dickens's *Pickwick Papers*. Mr. Pickwick has
just bumped into a character he had met earlier in his journeys, Mr.
Pott, a small-town newspaper editor. Mr. Pott asks if Pickwick has seen
some recent articles that appeared in his journal:

> "They appeared in the form of a copious review of a work on
> Chinese metaphysics, sir," said Pott.
>
> "Oh," observed Mr. Pickwick; "from your pen, I hope?"
>
> "From the pen of my critic, sir," rejoined Pott with dignity.
>
> "An abstruse subject I should conceive," said Mr. Pickwick.
>
> "Very, sir," responded Pott, looking intensely sage. "He
> crammed for it, to use a technical but expressive term; he read
> up for the subject, at my desire, in the Encyclopaedia Britan-
> nica."
>
> "Indeed!" said Mr. Pickwick; "I was not aware that that valu-
> able work contained any information respecting Chinese meta-
> physics."
>
> "He read, sir," rejoined Pott, laying his hand on Mr. Pickwick's
> knee, and looking round with a smile of intellectual superiority,
> "he read for metaphysics under the letter M, and for China
> under the letter C, and combined his information, sir."
>
> Mr. Pott's features assumed so much additional grandeur at the
> recollection of the power and research displayed in the learned
> effusions in question, that some minutes elapsed before Mr.
> Pickwick felt emboldened to renew the conversation.[10]

Like Mr. Pott's critic reading for metaphysics under the letter *m* and
for China under the letter *c* and then combining his information, the relationship of knowledge and teaching was conceptualized as learning
one's subject matter in one domain and one's teaching skills in another
and simply combining the two to make a competent teacher.

Even after Lee Shulman's influential attack on this approach,[11] one sees the ongoing power of the "old" model. We can, for example, read an op-ed piece in the *New York Times* by the distinguished academic Leon Botstein, president of Bard College, who argues:

> Teaching has failed to gain respect because our education schools have defined their subject matter as pedagogy. . . .
>
> Instead, we ought to educate and organize teachers according to the subject matter they teach. The high school mathematics teacher and the elementary school mathematics teacher should be taught by mathematicians and consider other mathematicians their colleagues. . . .
>
> Our universities and colleges have relegated the training of teachers to second-class enclaves in which the industry of education has flourished. We should disband the education schools and integrate teacher education into the core of the university.
>
> This would place teacher training under the aegis of the graduate schools of arts and sciences. We should eliminate the bachelor's degree in education and require teachers to have a degree in a subject other than education, and preferably in the subject the person intends to teach. . . . Classroom teaching skills can be taught in apprenticeship programs after a B.A. is completed, and on the job with close supervision.[12]

Now, John Dewey would agree with Botstein that teachers need to be "trained in the higher levels of intellectual method,"[13] but what Botstein misses is Dewey's great insight that only by looking at the subject matter *from the point of view of the student* (and not from the point of view of the academic discipline alone) will we have people who know how to teach others. Academic knowledge is a fine and important starting point, and some teachers and scholars manage almost by accident to turn that knowledge into good teaching of children or adults. But, Dewey urges:

> If some teachers, by sheer plenitude of knowledge, keep by instinct in touch with the mental activity of their pupils, and accomplish so much without, and even in spite of, principles which are theoretically sound, then there must be in this same

scholarship a tremendous resource when it is *more consciously used* [emphasis added].[14]

More "conscious use" in my mind means paying attention to the ways that we think about subject matter, how it is organized, and how students should and could be encountering it. We could, for example, consider the following scenario:

> A younger friend has just entered university and is required to take an introductory science course. Your friend does not know anything about the professors teaching the courses that could fulfill the requirement—except that one of those professors has won the Nobel Prize in physics. Do you advise your friend to take the course with the Nobel Prize winner? Yes or no?

When I have tried out this problem on people over the years, they can talk about the pros and cons of taking the course with the Nobel Prize winner. Usually, the responses on the positive side mention the fact that the Nobel Prize winner has a large command of the subject area, has a big-picture view, we might say. The Nobel Prize winner also has a certain kind of glamour, and studying with such a figure presents therefore certain kinds of psychic rewards for the student. (One might call this the "iconic" status of certain teachers.) On the negative side, respondents often mention the fact that the Nobel Prize winner may know *too* much about the field: he or she may have a level of specialized knowledge that makes it impossible to relate to a beginning student.

All these concerns—and others that are commonly raised—are true and legitimate, but what respondents rarely say is the key question that we need to answer in judging the success of the Nobel Prize winner as a teacher: How does the person think about the subject matter *in relation to the students being taught*? Let us consider what, in practice, this might mean. To my mind, thinking about the subject matter in relation to the students is expressed in two ways. First, the teacher—at whatever level in the educational system—needs to be thinking about one important question that I would express as, What's worth learning here? Second, once this question has been answered, teachers need to think about the "pedagogical content knowledge" that is required to enact the actual teaching. Let us look at each of these dimensions in turn.

What's Worth Learning Here?

In asking, What's worth learning here? I mean the following: for these students, in this setting, with these particular constraints of time and context—what should be taught? Not what *could* be taught, not what is the sum total about this subject area that I the teacher know, but what *should* be taught? How does this question get answered? I think it begins with envisioning the maximalist point of view about the subject matter being taught and moves from there through a series of "screens" to a realistic understanding of, What's worth learning here?[15] Another way to put the idea of the maximalist position is to ask a different but related question: What's *possible* to teach here? We can think of it as "the universe of possibilities" around any particular text. For example, say that we wanted to think about what's possible to teach about the following biblical text:

> Remember what Amalek did to you on your journey, after you left Egypt—how, undeterred by fear of God, he surprised you on the march, when you were famished and weary, and cut down all the stragglers in your rear. Therefore, when the Lord your God grants you safety from all your enemies around you, in the land that the Lord your God is giving you as a hereditary portion, you shall blot out the memory of Amalek from under heaven. Do not forget! (Deut. 25:17–19)

We might begin with the oddities of a text that talks about remembering and forgetting: the Israelites are enjoined to remember to blot out Amalek's memory. But wouldn't that very remembering constitute *not* blotting out that memory? What other things are possible to teach about this text? We might, for instance, consider comparing this text with other relevant biblical texts. The story of the attack of Amalek first appears in Exodus 17. It is possible to compare the two versions of the story. In addition, Amalek reappears in the dramatic story of Saul's war against the Amalek king Agag in 1 Samuel. There Saul is told by the prophet Samuel to "go attack Amalek, and proscribe all that belongs to him. Spare no one, but kill alike men and women, infants and sucklings, oxen and sheep, camels and asses" (1 Sam. 15:3). Saul's failure to do so leads to his loss of the kingship. The specter of Amalek returns once again in the Scroll of Esther, where Haman is identified as the "Agagite," a descendant of Agag, the Amalekite king (Esther 3:1).

Aside from these textual comparisons, there are other aspects to the "universe of possibilities" that a teacher might consider. The section from Deuteronomy quoted above appears, of course, in the annual liturgical reading of the Torah, in the reading known as *Ki tetze*. How is our understanding of this passage influenced by its context in that Torah-reading unit? How is our understanding affected by the immediate preceding verses, which deal with honest weights and measures? Rashi,[16] the great medieval exegete, offers a suggestion about that very question, and therefore at this point a teacher could fruitfully bring in Rashi's commentary. How does the context of the parallel passage in Exodus influence our understanding of the text? (There it appears immediately before the visit of Jethro and the revelation at Sinai, a very different moment in the biblical narrative.)

Other lines of inquiry might also be explored by the teacher. The passage from Deuteronomy has another liturgical function. It is a special reading always recited on the Sabbath immediately preceding the holiday of Purim. In doing so, another connection is made to the Esther story (read on Purim), but the relationship with Purim offers other pedagogic possibilities. The teacher might consider the image of Amalek in later rabbinic commentary and bring other texts to study. Amalek is associated in this literature with the enemies of Israel such as Rome, and that, too, affects our understanding of the text and how it might be taught. Surely, there are other possibilities as well. But the point is by now clear—there is a wide range of options, and some choices will have to be made. Amid all these possibilities, what should be taught?

Before reflecting on how such choices might be arrived at, I want to consider another question raised by the exploration above: How does a teacher even know the "universe of possibilities" in teaching any given subject area? It is clear that part of the answer must come from the experiences that teachers themselves have had when *they* were students. How had this text been taught to them, either as children or in more advanced courses they may have taken? After all, it is well known that the "apprenticeship of observation," the many years that teachers spend in classrooms in their youth, as students, later comes to have a profound impact on the way that they, in turn, will teach others.[17]

Obviously, a second way of developing the "universe of possibilities" comes from the teacher's own intelligence and ideas. Teachers read biblical texts, think about them, and invent their own readings and interpretations of these texts, quite independent of what they may have learned from their own teachers (although it is possible that teachers have learned not just specific ideas in their own studies, but more importantly, *ways of thinking* from these courses).

Finally, an underappreciated additional input can come from the teacher's reading of secondary scholarship and commentary. This in itself resembles an experience of sitting in a classroom with a teacher or scholar but doing it through reading rather than one's physical presence in that scholar's classroom. One could imagine, for example, a teacher wishing to teach the beginning of the Jacob and Esau narrative in Genesis 25 reading a few different approaches to understanding the text from the available secondary literature. A teacher may wish to look at the complex structural, compositional elements in this text. Such a teacher might turn to a classic work like E. A. Speiser's commentary on Genesis, found in the Anchor Bible series.[18] The teacher would want to look at the way that the *J* document and the *P* document intermingle in this text, about the "chronological chasm between the two versions" and the "wide gap in the motives that each gives for Jacob's departure."[19] This teacher might also be interested in the context of ancient biblical law, reading in Speiser that "business transactions in the Near East, while always subject to strict legal norms, have also been looked upon to some extent as a game, one in which contestants match wits with one another."[20] The teacher would try to bring relevant ancient Near Eastern documents to use for comparison so that "what's worth learning" would include a great deal about the context in which the Bible emerged.

The teacher might also be interested in knowing, by contrast, how this text was understood in the early days of the formation of rabbinic culture. Turning to James Kugel's *The Bible As It Was*,[21] one would learn that the image of the biblical Esau was "modified by early interpreters. . . . He became utterly wicked, a crafty, bloodthirsty embodiment of evil."[22] Why did this happen? Kugel explains:

> Part of the motive for this change is to be found in the later history of Israel, as reflected in the Bible itself. After all, Esau was the ancestor of the Edomites, Israel's close neighbor and sometimes fierce enemy. Later biblical texts frequently heaped scorn on the Edomites, and sometimes this scorn was couched in terms that reflected back on the founder of that nation.[23]

A teacher could turn to the texts cited in Kugel's volume to use in class as a way of indicating the ancient interpretive traditions about Jacob and Esau.

By contrast yet again, a teacher could consider a literary analysis of the story. Robert Alter, for example, reads this text in a very different way—not so much as a "collision of national archetypes" but as a complex presentation of the story's "personages in the fullness of a mature fictional imagination."[24] For Alter, Jacob's "prudent" concern about the future "qualifies him as a suitable bearer of the birthright: historical destiny does not just happen; you have to know how to make it happen, how to keep your eye on the distant horizon of present events."[25] But this very quality is also, in Alter's eyes, viewed with ambivalence by the biblical text, which "may even raise some moral questions about him."[26] A teacher who decides to use Alter's focus for pedagogical purposes—as a gauge of "what's worth learning here"—would want to emphasize these very ambivalences and find ways for students to discover the interesting nuances in the text that Alter uncovers.

These three examples above are among many that teachers could use as resources in guiding teaching. My point is that, along with the teacher's own native intelligence and academic background, scholarly sources provide an opportunity for further pedagogic sophistication.[27]

Finally, the "universe of possibilities" needs to be filtered through other screens. As I have pointed out earlier in this book, time is the constant counterpoint to all teaching. We as teachers are always challenged by the constraints of time to edit down what we are doing. Time is only one element of the "milieu" in which teaching takes place. We need also to take into account the physical environment in which learning takes place, the ideological framework of the institution, and the larger elements of the communal "milieu" that I have explored at the beginning of this book. Moreover, even if all those factors could be ruled out, we would still need to screen out some of those "possibilities" simply because of our own sense of goals—what matters to us personally—and, perhaps even more importantly, how we understand who the learners are. What backgrounds do they bring with them? What are they interested in learning? What are they capable of learning? These questions are only some of the issues that would need to be addressed.

The process of moving from the world of possibility to the world of practical teaching that I have tried to explore above can be represented in a more direct visual way by the following chart:

The Relationship between Subject-Matter Knowledge and What Gets Taught

A Look at Planning for Teaching

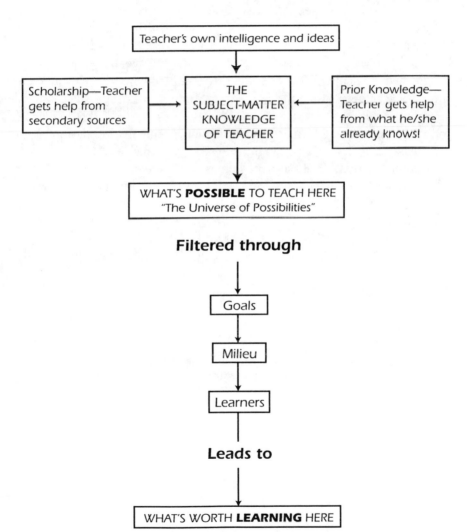

Pedagogical Content Knowledge

Preconceptions and Difficulties

Once the teacher has dealt with the question of "what's worth learning here," the second dimension of planning for teaching involves working on the pedagogical content knowledge required to conceptualize the teaching and learning experience. "Pedagogical content knowledge," as I have discussed earlier in this book, is the term that Lee Shulman and his students and colleagues have used to describe the meeting place between knowledge of subject matter and knowledge of learners. How might pedagogical content knowledge be implemented in real-life planning for teaching? Using the issues that Shulman has suggested,[28] I conceptualize this implementation as a two-step process. First, the teacher needs to imagine the "situation" of his or her students in relation to the particular text that will be taught. No student comes as a *tabula rasa* to the potential text. Each student comes with previous knowledge and with certain preconceptions or misconceptions about the biblical text. Not only that but, as I have indicated in chapter 5, texts present certain difficulties of various sorts. Teachers need to try to imagine what those difficulties might be. As a teacher, I find it helpful to ask myself a set of questions to help clarify this aspect of pedagogical content knowledge. The same questions obtain whether the students are beginners or advanced; I think about them when I teach graduate students or rabbinical students, children, adolescents, or adult learners.

I begin by asking myself what *I* find difficult in this text. What perplexes me, what puzzles me about the language, the grammatical structures, the historical and contextual background of the text, the philosophical difficulties, and the "mindset" of the text, if we can use that term? My own difficulties are important to clarify, but they are also important to distinguish from what my students will experience. Certainly, that is true when teaching children, but even when teaching adults or experienced students, I have to know the difference between what is *my* difficulty and what is theirs.

For example, in the Deuteronomy text about Amalek quoted above, the notion of blotting out the memory of Amalek may be less troubling to me than it will be to another learner. After many years of engagement with the Bible, I am prepared to accept the gaps in worldview between the Bible and me. Adolescents may be less willing to do so. Learners coming to the serious study of the Bible in adulthood may also be less forgiving. Teachers who don't distinguish between their own questions and their students' are likely to encounter unwelcome surprises in teaching. They won't be prepared for a student to ask, "Well, who did Cain marry if Cain and Abel were Adam and Eve's only children?" or, "Why does the Bible say the world was created in six days when we know that science has a very different view?"

Mature readers of the Bible may have long ago solved these problems for themselves and may rarely, if ever, think about them. But the difference between readers and *teachers* of the Bible is that teachers must always keep the questions of potential learners in mind, even when the teacher may no longer share the same questions. One teacher related the following experience:

> I was preparing to teach a group of twenty-somethings the story of the Exodus and the crossing of the sea (Exodus 14). These were learners who had found their way back to the Bible after various detours through "spiritual seeking"—Eastern religions, etc. I walked into class well prepared to deal with the question that I anticipated would be most on their minds, namely, the miracle of the splitting of the sea and how we could understand that today. I had photocopied Buber's definition of miracle,[29] I had read Moshe Greenberg's discussion of miracle,[30] I had read Ruth Zielenziger's presentation in the Melton teacher's guide[31]— but when I actually came to this section in the text, no one raised any questions! I was shocked. I asked them, so what do you think about this splitting of the sea? And they answered, "It's a miracle—what's the problem?" I had not taken into consideration at all that *my* difficulties with miracles were not *their* difficulties with miracles. Having been through the spiritual supermarket of contemporary America, they found it perfectly acceptable to believe in miracles. For me, an old-fashioned religious *rationalist*, miracles were a problem that had to be solved. For them, the Bible was a miraculous story to be believed.

Veteran teachers, reflecting on their experiences teaching particular texts over the course of time with many different students, begin to develop their own file folder of typical questions and difficulties. They learn to recognize the kinds of misconceptions that students walk into class with, and though the teacher will sometimes be wrong, the weight of experience will more often than not help give preparation for what is likely to be encountered. Indeed, one of the reasons that "reflective practice" has become such an important dimension of teacher education is precisely because of its power in helping teachers prepare for "the next time" a text will be taught.[32] To sum up what has been stated so far, a teacher needs to think about the following:

---

1. What do you, the teacher, find difficult or confusing in the text?
2. What in this text will your potential students find difficult?
3. What preconceptions (prior beliefs) will your potential students bring with them?
4. What misconceptions (errors) will your potential students bring with them?

Of course, dealing with preconceptions and difficulties is not the only element involved in planning for teaching. Earlier, we looked at the question of "what's worth learning here," and perhaps we could say that every teaching experience is some combination of both sides of this coin—what students come in with (preconceptions, misconceptions, and difficulties) and what you, the teacher, want them to walk away with. We could characterize this latter point with its own question:

What key ideas, practices, or values would you want to teach those students about this text?

Representations

Above, I said that implementing pedagogical content knowledge involves a two-step process. If the analysis of preconceptions and difficulties (combined with "what's worth learning here?") could be considered the "inputs" in planning teaching, the "outputs" are the "representations" of the subject that allow students to understand what is being presented and how their difficulties and preconceptions are being addressed.

"Representations" is a term used by contemporary education scholars to mean "a wide range of models that may convey something about the subject matter to the learner: activities, questions, examples, and analogies, for instance."[33] Thus, the teacher needs to think about the various means by which problems will be addressed and goals for learning will be attained. What will students do in the class today to help them understand the text? How will I find an analogy to deal with the problem of blotting out the name of Amalek? (Do I draw comparisons to Hitler here?) How will I communicate the power of memory, as it is expressed in that text? (Do I make connections to the students' own personal memories, or does that trivialize the Bible or misrepresent it?) What are the "partial translations" that need to be made here (to use Rosenak's term, discussed in chapter 5)?[34] The task for a teacher, then, is to answer the following:

> What examples, analogies, anecdotes, stories, demonstrations, explanations, or visual representations might you use to:
>
> a) deal with the preconceptions/misconceptions of students
> b) communicate the core of what you want to teach

As suggested in my question earlier, however, not all representations represent the subject matter well. Some misrepresent the text, usually in ways unanticipated by the teacher. In one study, for example, the researcher saw a biology teacher represent photosynthesis by an analogy to plants eating. However,

> [a]lthough this seems intuitively appealing, Roth's work on pupils' misconceptions about photosynthesis makes one realize that another analogy might be a better choice. Each alternative must be evaluated carefully however. . . . Knowing that analogies can be useful pedagogical devices does not help the beginning teacher answer [questions about which representation to use].[35]

The challenges presented to teachers—particularly, inexperienced teachers—about constructing appropriate representations are immense. These issues led me, earlier in this book, to muse about creating a "Bible genome project,"[36] an attempt to map out the full range of approaches, theories, practices, and pedagogies for teaching the Bible. Such a project, I imagined, would aim to help teachers deal with representations in a more effective and rigorous fashion. But of course, any such program is only a fantasy, because of the vast enterprise involved and because of the difficulties in even defining the terrain and questions to be explored. For example, how would we organize the biblical texts under consideration—by the order in which the Bible is arranged, starting with Genesis and ending with Chronicles? Or would we consider the Bible according to genre—working out theories and practices for biblical narrative, poetry, law, and so on? Or would there be other forms of organization that could be imagined (such as by order of pedagogic difficulty)?

But with all the above being noted, I think it is impossible to imagine a way to transform the "genome project" into an essential element of teacher education. I could picture an extended exercise that seems to me to be quite powerful, offering a good deal of potential to improve teaching. It would be one way, among many, that could help teachers work on their own practice and do better planning about what they are teaching. Teacher education, argue Lampert and Ball, "must seek to prepare teachers to reason wisely, to develop courses of action in response to particulars, to extend and improvise beyond that which they have acquired or done before."[37] I imagine the modified genome exercise as a significant activity in teacher learning—either in teacher preparation programs or in professional development programs offered in in-service education. Let me suggest one possible model.

I would begin where I began earlier in this chapter, using the exercises about what's worth learning here and exploring afterward the needed pedagogical content knowledge that emanates out of that exploration. A group of prospective teachers in a teacher preparation program (or experienced teachers in a professional development program) would take a biblical text, and brainstorm what might be central to the text ("what's worth learning here") and what might be problematic in that text. These prospective teachers would first attempt to answer those "problems" for themselves and then think about how they might "represent" them for children.

At that point, they would turn to Bible scholars for help. They would explore with these scholars the same questions about centrality and potential problems. Because "we cannot simply treat knowledge as being more or less general, without considering the class of situations across which we want knowledge to transfer,"[38] I would then ask our participants (future teachers or teachers from the field) to go to real schools and watch classes encountering the biblical text that our group is working on. Keeping in mind their own explorations of the biblical text under consideration and their interviews with Bible scholars, they would analyze questions raised by students in the classes being observed. They would compare the questions of students with their own questions and the Bible scholars' questions. To get a better understanding of what is going on in the minds of the learners, our participants would then interview the students whom they have observed. They would interview the teachers whom they have just watched to get a different perspective on the same questions. They would want to find out from these teachers what real-life problems of practice they have encountered and learn about their successful (and unsuccessful!) representations. (This is what Shulman has called learning from "the wisdom of practice.")[39]

After accumulating all these data, our participants would then try to construct representations, working in groups and trying the representations out on one another. They would take these representations to the Bible scholars for reactions and analysis. They would want the scholars to think about ways that these new representations do or do not represent the subject matter accurately. Of course, in the spirit of Joseph Schwab's work on the process of curriculum development, we would want to them to be cautious about the tyranny of the subject-matter experts in matters of education. As Schwab put it: "It is easy for the scholar-specialist to overawe the group and to impose the character and structure of his discipline as the correct model for the character and structure of the curriculum."[40]

So we would want our participants to decide how seriously to take the scholars' reactions, in the light of what our teachers have seen in their observations of children or in their knowledge of the specific milieus in which these lessons will be actualized. Finally, we would want our work to be tried out in classrooms with real students, taught both by our participants and by other teachers who were not part of the process that they have gone through. At the end, we would evaluate the entire experience and try to determine what we had learned.

By spending time with both peers and scholars, our participants would have a chance to delve into the biblical subject matter with depth and in the spirit of careful inquiry and analysis. On the other side, giving them a chance to observe actual teaching practice would lead them to what is the ultimate goal of teacher education, what Deborah Ball and David Cohen have called "learning professional performance." As they explain:

> To learn anything relevant to performance, professionals need experience with the tasks and ways of thinking that are fundamental to the practice. Those experiences must be immediate enough to be compelling and vivid. To learn more than mere imitation or survival, such experiences also must be sufficiently

distanced to be open to careful scrutiny, unpacking, reconstruction and the like.[41]

Now, it's unlikely (to say the least) that we could do such a process with every piece of text that teachers will teach, but we could use this as a model for the kind of preparation that teachers—ideally—would do in preparing any piece of text for students. With that model in mind, teachers would be challenged to refine their pedagogic thinking and make their preparation a serious intellectual enterprise. Ball has noted that making the moves that take one from knowledge of the subject to structuring learning experiences for others involves complex thinking. Among other things, it requires "the capacity to deconstruct one's own knowledge into a less polished and final form, where critical components are accessible and visible."[42] A polished knowledge of subject matter may actually inhibit thinking about how others may learn what you already know. Even the outwardly simple task of offering an explanation only will work with learners "if it is at a sufficient level of granularity, that is, if it includes in it the steps necessary for the reasoning to make sense for a particular learner or a whole class, based on what they currently know or do not know."[43]

Teaching the Bible, of course, encompasses a good deal more than good preparation and intellectual inquiry. This book has addressed only some of the important issues embodied in our work. Knowledge of students, opportunities for supervision, mentorships, and what Magdalene Lampert has termed "the development of a discourse of practice"[44] are all elements in growing as a teacher. In addition, I have not at all addressed the moral dimension of the act of teaching, the way that my behavior as a teacher—the way that I relate to students as persons—is a profound and compelling issue, especially with Bible as the subject matter.[45] Aside from that, I have not dealt with the day-to-day quality of teaching that is perhaps its most persistent feature.[46]

Teaching is an uncertain practice.[47] Its uncertainties have to do with our imperfect understanding of our students and what they need and, indeed, of what they are learning at all. Even its subject matter is uncertain. When I say Bible, what Bible do I really mean? What does my school mean, and what do my students think I mean?

Perhaps most of all, its uncertainty has to do with the ever changing and unpredictable nature of the encounters that occur every day in the classroom. I can never really predict what my students will say, even with material that I have taught many times. From year to year, from

day to day there are surprises. Of course, this is one of the great pleasures of teaching, but just as surely it produces its greatest anxieties.

"Adventurous" teaching is what we wish to do and what we wish
to see in others.[48] Much of that adventure will occur in the unpredictable daily encounters that we will experience with our students—
how we negotiate their concerns, how we address their questions, how
we respond to their dilemmas. The challenge before us lies in turning
our knowledge into teaching, taking our goals and seeing them realized,
and making the difficult transitions from theory to practice.

Looking back over this book, I worry that I have been perhaps too
cavalier about moving from thinking to action, from the world of ideas
to the realities of practical teaching. How we make those moves is a
complex activity—uncertain, true, but immensely rewarding. All that,
however, will have to wait for another time. Perhaps, as Buber said, in
words that we looked at in the previous chapter, what matters most is
"readiness." For now, I hope, we have at least begun.

Notes

1. John Dewey, "The Relation of Theory to Practice," in *John Dewey on Education,* ed. Reginald D. Archambault (Chicago: University of Chicago Press,
   1964), p. 318.
2. Ibid., pp. 320–21.
3. Ibid., p. 321.
4. I have discussed the work of Shulman and some of his colleagues and students
   in chap. 2 of this volume.
5. Philip W. Jackson, *Life in Classrooms* (New York: Holt, Rinehart and Winston,
   1968), p. 152.
6. Lee Shulman has described this process as the "cycle" that connects "pedagogical reasoning" and action in his "Knowledge and Teaching: Foundations of the
   New Reform," *Harvard Educational Review* 57, no. 1 (February 1987): 1–22.
7. Sharon Feiman-Nemser and Margret Buchmann, "The First Year of Teacher
   Preparation: Transition to Pedagogical Thinking," *Journal of Curriculum Studies* 18, no. 3 (1986): 239.
8. See Pamela L. Grossman, Suzanne M. Wilson, and Lee S. Shulman, "Teachers of
   Substance: Subject-Matter Knowledge for Teaching," in *Knowledge Base for the
   Beginning Teacher,* ed. M. Reynolds (New York: Pergamon, 1989), pp. 23–36.
9. Ruth M. Heaton and Magdalene Lampert, "Learning to Hear Voices: Inventing
   a New Pedagogy of Teacher Education," in *Teaching for Understanding: Challenges for Policy and Practice,* ed. David K. Cohen, Milbrey W. McLaughlin,
   and Joan E. Talbert (San Francisco: Jossey-Bass, 1993), p. 49.

10. Charles Dickens, *The Pickwick Papers* (London: Penguin, 1972), p. 815.

11. See Shulman's "Those Who Understand: Knowledge Growth in Teaching," *Educational Researcher* 15, no. 2 (1986): 4–14, and his "Knowledge and Teaching."

12. Leon Botstein, "Making the Teaching Profession Respectable Again," *New York Times*, 26 July 1999.

13. Dewey, "The Relation of Theory to Practice," p. 328.

14. Ibid., p. 330.

15. The perspective offered here, as is obvious, owes a great deal to Ralph Tyler, who uses the term "screen" as a mode of developing curricular objectives in his classic work *Basic Principles of Curriculum and Instruction* (Chicago: University of Chicago Press, 1949). Tyler's work, though very relevant to the specific needs of teachers, is focused most directly on the institution's educational program as a whole. In addition, the screens used by Tyler differ from what I have proposed here. Joseph Schwab's work in curriculum is also relevant here, though it, too, focuses less on the individual teacher than on the larger educational system. See his "The Practical 3: Translation into Curriculum" (1973), in his collected essays, *Science, Curriculum, and Liberal Education,* ed. Ian Westbury and Neil J. Wilkof (Chicago: University of Chicago Press, 1978), pp. 365–83. See also my "Making 'The Practical' Real: The Experience of the Melton Research Center in Curriculum Design" [in Hebrew], *Studies in Jewish Education* 6 (1992): 196–200.

16. Rabbi Shlomo Yitzhaki, 1040–1105.

17. Dan C. Lortie, *Schoolteacher: A Sociological Study* (Chicago: University of Chicago Press, 1975), pp. 61–67.

18. E. A. Speiser, *Genesis,* Anchor Bible 1 (Garden City, N.Y.: Doubleday, 1964).

19. Ibid., p. 215.

20. Ibid., p. 196.

21. James L. Kugel, *The Bible As It Was* (Cambridge, Mass.: Belknap Press of Harvard University Press, 1997).

22. Ibid., p. 202.

23. Ibid.

24. Robert Alter, *The Art of Biblical Narrative* (New York: Basic Books, 1981), p. 43.

25. Ibid., p. 45.

26. Ibid.

27. See also Joseph Lukinsky, "Jewish Education and Jewish Scholarship: Maybe the Lies We Tell Are Really True," in *The Seminary at 100,* ed. Nina Beth Cardin and David Wolf Silverman (New York: Rabbinical Assembly and Jewish Theological Seminary, 1987), pp. 205–14.

28. See n. 11 above.

29. From Martin Buber, *Moses: The Revelation and the Covenant* (New York: Harper & Row, 1958), pp. 75–77.

30. Moshe Greenberg, "On Teaching the Bible in Religious Schools," *Jewish Education* 29, no. 3 (1959): 45–53.

31. Ruth Zielenziger, *Exodus: A Teacher's Guide* (New York: Melton Research Center, 1984), p. 131.
32. To choose just one of many examples, see Renee T. Clift, W. Robert Houston, and Marleen C. Pugach, eds., *Encouraging Reflective Practice in Education* (New York: Teachers College Press, 1990).
33. G. Williamson McDiarmid, Deborah Loewenberg Ball, and Charles W. Anderson, "Why Staying One Chapter Ahead Doesn't Really Work: Subject-Specific Pedagogy," in *Knowledge Base for the Beginning Teacher*, ed. Reynolds, p. 194. Also: Shulman, "Those Who Understand," p. 6.
34. Michael Rosenak, *Roads to the Palace: Jewish Texts and Teaching* (Providence: Berghahn, 1995).
35. McDiarmid et al., "Why Staying One Chapter Ahead Doesn't Really Work," p. 195. The article refers to the work of K. J. Roth, "Conceptual Change Learning and Student Processing of Science Texts" (Ph.D. diss., Michigan State University, 1985).
36. See chap. 2 of this volume.
37. Magdalene Lampert and Deborah Loewenberg Ball, *Teaching, Multimedia, and Mathematics: Investigations of Real Practice* (New York: Teachers College Press, 1998), p. 36.
38. Ibid., p. 30. They are referring to the work on "situated learning" done by Greeno, Smith, and Moore.
39. Shulman, "Those Who Understand," p. 10.
40. Schwab, "The Practical 3," p. 368.
41. Deborah Loewenberg Ball and David K. Cohen, "Developing Practice, Developing Practitioners: Toward a Practice-Based Theory of Professional Education," in *Teaching as the Learning Profession: Handbook of Policy and Practice*, ed. Gary Sykes and Linda Darling-Hammond (San Francisco: Jossey-Bass, 1999), p. 12.
42. Deborah Loewenberg Ball, "Bridging Practices: Intertwining Content and Pedagogy in Teaching and Learning to Teach," *Journal of Teacher Education* 51, no. 3 (May/June 2000): 245.
43. Ibid.
44. Magdalene Lampert, "Knowing Teaching from the Inside Out: Implications of Inquiry in Practice for Teacher Education," in *The Education of Teachers*, ed. Gary A. Griffin, *Ninety-Eighth Yearbook of the National Society for the Study of Education* (NSSE), pt. 1 (Chicago: University of Chicago Press: 1999), p. 170.
45. See, for example, Christopher M. Clark, *Thoughtful Teaching* (New York: Teachers College Press, 1995), pp. 19–32; and Alan R. Tom, *Teaching as a Moral Craft* (New York: Longman, 1984).
46. What Jackson, in *Life in Classrooms*, called "the daily grind."
47. Joseph P. McDonald, *Teaching: Making Sense of an Uncertain Craft* (New York: Teachers College Press, 1992); Lampert and Ball, *Teaching, Multimedia, and*

Mathematics, esp. pp. 23–37; and Deborah Loewenberg Ball and Suzanne M. Wilson, "Integrity in Teaching: Recognizing the Fusion of the Moral and Intellectual," *American Educational Research Journal* 33, no. 1 (spring 1996): 155–96.

48. David K. Cohen, "Practice and Policy: Notes on the History of Instruction," in *American Teachers: Histories of a Profession at Work,* ed. Donald Warren (New York: Macmillan, 1993). Also: Cohen et al., *Teaching for Understanding* (see n. 9 above).

Index